The *Horse of Course!* GUIDE to WINNING the WESTERN TRAIL CLASS

Diane Adair takes Fancy Pants over a practice jump.

The *Horse of Course!* GUIDE to WINNING the WESTERN TRAIL CLASS

LYNDA BLOOM

ARCO PUBLISHING, INC.
NEW YORK

Published by Arco Publishing, Inc.
219 Park Avenue South, New York, N.Y. 10003

Copyright © 1977, 1978, 1979, 1980, 1981, 1982

by Derbyshire Publishing Co., Inc.

Library of Congress Cataloging in Publication Data

Bloom, Lynda.
   The Horse of course! guide to winning the Western
trail class.

   Articles from Horse, of course!
   Includes index.
   1. Trail horse class.   2. Horse-training.
I. Greene, Russell A., 1930–   II. Horse, of course!
III. Title.   IV. Title: Guide to winning the Western
trail class.
SF296.T7B58   636.1'08'88   78-13541

ISBN 0-668-04569-8 (Cloth Edition)

Printed in the United States of America

THIS BOOK IS DEDICATED TO THE MEMORY
OF KATHY CROMWELL'S ONCE-IN-A-LIFETIME
TRAIL HORSE MARE, *Opie's Misty*

Contents

Preface

In early 1971, Dr. R. A. Greene, a veterinarian and Quarter Horse breeder, became convinced that there was a definite need for a new type of horse publication, one that got down to basics and translated the jargon of the professionals into plain English that people could understand and use.

As he tells it, "I didn't know anything about magazine publishing, but I had over forty years of experience with horses as a breeder, trainer, showman and veterinarian. Yet, with all my experience, I still had trouble understanding some of the how-to-do-it articles appearing in the existing horse publications. I reasoned that there must be many other people having the same problem, so I decided to start a magazine that I knew would appeal to me in the hope that it would appeal to them."

Midway through 1971, Dr. Greene was severely kicked by a reluctant patient and during his long period of convalescence he began to develop his idea of the perfect horse magazine. He asked for comments and suggestions from his horse-owning friends. Eventually one wing of the main horse barn on his Derbyshire Farm was converted into editorial offices for the production of the proposed magazine.

In January of 1972, the first issue of HORSE OF COURSE!, as it was named, went into the mail. The first issue had a paid circulation of only 109 paid subscribers . . . a rather modest beginning. Within five years over 125,000 families were paying to receive it each month. Obviously, there were many horse people who shared Dr. Greene's concept of the ideal horse magazine.

In order to insure an adequate supply of appropriate "how-to" editorial material for HORSE OF COURSE!, several of the leading photo-journalists serving the horse field were commissioned to write complete books devoted to a specific area of horse ownership, training, or riding. They were instructed to assume no previous horse knowledge on the part of the reader and to be certain that the combination of words and photos would permit *anyone* to understand and use the contents of their books. It was understood that each chapter would stand alone as an article, but when all of those articles were combined, they would constitute the most comprehensive treatment of the subject available in print.

You are now holding one of those books.

The *Horse of Course!* GUIDE to WINNING the WESTERN TRAIL CLASS

Chapter One

Training Strategy for the Western Trail Horse

The two most important ingredients in training a trail horse are PATIENCE and GOOD SENSE. Without these, you'll produce a horse that blows up each time it sees an obstacle. You have to give your horse a chance to be good. You have to be sure that he's *ready* for the schooling, and you have to think out every phase of his training. One mistake could cost you months of work. First on the list of "thought" is a look into the subject of how ready the horse is.

Trail-training is advantageous to people "bored" with raising colts, because it is quite possible to start a little basic work, such as simple stepovers, with a young horse. We had a weanling last year who, within two weeks of being halter broke at age six months, was walking a row of tires, doing simple stepovers, and calmly going over a teetering bridge. This was one of the most brilliant prospects I've seen because he had the MIND for it and he liked doing it. He also remembered each lesson well. The first time he was introduced to a car tire, he was led up and I placed each of his front feet in the tire center, then had him stand there a while, while he was petted and

1.1. PATIENCE *and* GOOD SENSE *are the two most important ingredients in training any trail horse.*

praised. From then on, he could be led up to any tire anywhere, even a larger tractor tire, and he'd step right in, dead
center in the rim and stand there and wait to get petted! If
they were all like this, trail-training would be a cinch—but
they're not.

We had a weanling filly by the same sire as this colt, and
she was "in a hurry" all the time. By age two, she was quieter
and could have accepted simple stepovers or tires. As a weanling, however, she would have blown up and been ready for
a fight if asked to place her feet in a tire or walk slowly over
a log.

These two horses illustrate just how different trail-horse
prospects can be. Some are ready to fool with at an early age,
others need more maturity. Some never make it. It's up to you
to determine if you can take your young horse before it's old
enough to ride and give it an introduction to simple stepovers.

How about a broke horse? How "broke" should it be before
you start it on obstacles? You can do your basic ground-work
whether or not the horse is green or finished, but before you
start riding him on backthroughs, or sidepasses, or any of the
"control" obstacles, you'd better be sure he has enough *handle*
and coordination to accept all this. Chapter Three will tell you
how to teach the control movements you need to have on a
horse before riding him on any obstacles that require them.
But, before that, you should have your horse broke enough
that he gives his head to you easily, backs easily, responds to
some leg pressure and can turn around. He needs to know the
meaning of "whoa" and he must respect it. If you're riding a
green colt that still can't walk a straight line or turn around in
less than a half-acre, you can't expect him to get it all together to work an obstacle. Simple stepovers would be in his
repertoire, but anything requiring turning or body control
wouldn't be.

PUNISHMENT

How to punish, when to do it, and where to do it are things you MUST think about about before you start, lest you ruin your trail horse. Some riders are in such a hurry that they put a horse before difficult obstacles too soon. When the horse blows up from lack of understanding, the rider blows up and begins taking it out on the horse. First, be sure you have a REASON to punish the horse. Punishment takes on many forms. It can be simply restriction. If the horse approaches an obstacle too fast, or does something such as stepping on the rim of the tire when he has been TAUGHT from the ground to step in the center and knows better than to hit the rim, you have reason to punish. This restriction punishment is done very calmly and simply. You quietly back the horse up, any-where from a few feet to several yards and try it again. The horse is not rattled, and YOU are not rattled and it was all done quietly. If he rushes again, or steps on a tire rim (these are just random examples of several instances where this pun-ishment applies), then you back him again. It won't take him long to realize that he doesn't get to go forward and "get it all over with" unless he does it right.

There will be times when you'll want to use your whip, or your heels, or your reins to punish a horse, but you have to be sure you do this correctly IF the horse has it coming. Perhaps he's being piggy and just doesn't want to do something unless you MAKE him do it.

A lot of horses are this way. *The worst thing you can do, however, is punish the horse at the obstacle.* ALWAYS TAKE THE HORSE AWAY FROM THE OBSTACLE IF YOU HAVE REASON TO GET AFTER HIM. If you spur a horse or whack him with a crop while he's working (or trying NOT to work) an obstacle, he's going to get rattled each time he approaches that obstacle because he thinks he's going to get in trouble. The thing to do is take him *away* from it and get his attention. This is much different from the "restriction punishment" and you use this more when the horse is being downright sour and knows better than to be lazy. Let's look at an example of this type of punishment.

A Paint mare we had was becoming a pretty fair trail horse as far as stepovers, pivots, and backthroughs. She didn't like sidepassing, though, and her attitude was, "I'm only going to sidepass this thing if you MAKE me do it." She had been thoroughly taught to sidepass away from obstacles before she was ever put on one, so she definitely knew how to do it. Quite often, after she was started on simple sidepasses, she would balk, pin her ears back and refuse to work the sidepass. She was a mare that was a little "silly" and had she gotten whacked at the obstacle, would have become an idiot at it from then on. Rather than get after her there, I would ride her away from all obstacles, take her out in the open, and give her one good whack on the rear end with the romel if she refused to sidepass. When I punish a horse, I don't make a big deal out of it. One good whack and strong leg pressure was all it took to convince her she'd better sidepass, or else. I can't see beating on a horse for fifteen minutes straight, as I've seen some people do, if you can get the point across with one or two good whacks. This way, you don't upset the horse, you just wake him up and get his attention. When this mare was taken back to the sidepass, nine out of ten times she'd work it, but if she didn't, we went back to the field for "a discussion." It never took more than two trips to the field, and before long, she decided it would save a lot of steps and a lot of hide if she just worked the sidepasses as well as she worked everything else.

BALKY HORSES get that way fast when they find out they can stop and outpull you if you try to lead them over something they don't want to step or jump over. We also have one like this in the barn. Now, he has had enough confidence in-

1.2. A horse has to be "ready" and in the right frame of mind to accept training for a Western trail class. You have to carefully think out each phase of his training.

stilled in him that he knows I will never take him to any obstacle that will hurt him. His problem is that he "tries" the
handler. I think he'll overcome this eventually and be a good
trail horse, but for now, he needs some "encouragement." For
example, he simply didn't like to work leadover jumps. They
were low, and easy, but he figured that unless someone was
behind him as well as in front, he didn't have to do anything
but stand there and rest. Having someone behind to cluck to
a horse and get him to take the jump is fine, and we sometimes
use this for a short period of time, but what you're after is to
get the horse to respond to the "person at the end of the rope."
If you're in a class at a show and you have a leadover jump
and your horse has found out at home that he can balk, he'll
quickly see that nobody is behind to help you get him over the
jump, so he's sure not going to take it.

I like to school balky horses with a halter. Some need a
chain shank, but what I found to work on our balker was a simple cotton lead rope. It was snapped to the ring on the right
side of the halter, brought under his chin and came out the
ring on the left side. The usual method I use in leadover jumps
is to walk up and make the horse stand until I step over myself
and with a LOOSE lead shank (to keep from jerking his head
during the jump) I cluck to him and ask him to come over.
Our balker would just stand there or take a few steps back. He
wasn't rattled, or trying to spook, he was just being balky. The
rope I use is at least ten feet long so I can move the horse back
some without having to come back over to his side of the jump.
Without actually jerking on his head, which would rattle him,
I took hold of the rope with both hands and did a strong
downward pull. This made the rope "take hold" of his chin
and he'd flip his head up and take a couple of steps back, but
he wasn't becoming rattled as he would have if a series of jerks
were done at his head. The one pull would get a reaction and
the instant I got it, I LOOSENED the rope and didn't tighten

it again unless a second pull was necessary. More often than not, I could stand on the other side of the jump (out of his way, of course) holding the rope completely loose and talk him over with a few simple sentences of, "You can do this, you know." Talking to a horse helps, though some trainers might disagree. If you can talk a horse into doing something, you can get him to do it without rattling him. By talking and holding a loose rope, you can get him to come right on over the jump. It won't always be instantaneous, but if you stand there long enough and let him think about what you did to him with the rope, he'll more than likely get sick of standing and come over for you. If you get one good jump, QUIT and put him away knowing he did it right. If you think about this, he had his ideas "reinforced" at the obstacle, but wasn't really punished, as he would have been had he been whacked with a whip or had his head repeatedly jerked.

What I hope these cases illustrate is the THOUGHT you must put into your punishment. There is a definite difference between actual punishment and the restriction or reinforcement punishment. You should never really *punish* the horse at the obstacle, but you can find other ways to get him to react. All you should ask is that he TRIES for you and forgets his bad attitude, then he should be put away happy as a reward.

Confidence . . . The Name of the Game

One of the worst things you can do is put a horse at too difficult an obstacle too soon in his training. As the saying goes, you have to learn to walk before you can run, and this certainly applies to trail horses. If you've ever seen a novice rider introducing his horse to stepovers by taking him right over a series of big logs, then you've seen a horse tripping and banging his legs against the logs and losing confidence. If an obstacle hurts a horse, he's not going to trust it anymore, nor will he trust YOU because you put him over it.

1.3. Confidence is the name of the game. You can't put a green horse through or over a difficult obstacle that can hurt him. You have to increase the demands you put on a trail horse gradually— you have to have the horse's confidence.

Think carefully about the meaning of the word "gradual." A "gradual" buildup of difficulty on something like stepovers means just that. It doesn't mean that today you step over one log three times, and tomorrow you do a series of twelve. It means that you might have to spend days, even weeks, working that single log. Then, you introduce a second log and spend days on that before you put another one before the horse. How fast you can progress depends on your horse's athletic ability, his mind, and his ability to concentrate. If he's worried about three or four poles ahead of him, he'll start flubbing at the first one. Coordination comes with practice, and confidence comes with "gradual" work.

1.4. When training a horse, move the obstacles around. Vary the course so that it appears to be entirely different each time you work a horse.

SHOW YOUR HORSE WHAT YOU WANT HIM TO DO.
Do it yourself. If you want him to walk over a pole, walk over
it in front of him, just as you want him to do it. If you walk
around it and expect him to walk *over* it, he's going to sense
something fishy. If he sees you step over it, though, he'll think,
"If it's good enough for a person, it's good enough for me—so
it must be safe." If you want him to go over a jump from the
ground-work, step over it yourself. Don't walk around it and
ask him to jump. If you want him to step into a water box, get
your feet wet. While you can't both stand in a tire at the same
time, there's not any reason why you can't step into it as you
lead in front of him, just before you want him to work it. All
this builds CONFIDENCE and makes a sort of a game out of
the schooling. You'll find a lot of good trail horses are horses
that like being handled and enjoy being around people.
They're real characters, so they naturally enjoy this type of
schooling.

REPETITION AND OVERWORK: THINGS TO AVOID

Horses get bored fast. If you spend seven days a week walking over the same poles, or backing an L in the same direction,
you accomplish two things you can do without. First, you get
a horse so used to working "one way" that he can't accept
change. Secondly, you bore him to death and he'll quickly
become sloppy over the obstacle because he's sick of looking
and working at it. We find it best to work obstacles only two
or three times a week for short periods of time. It keeps the
horse interested. We change the obstacles around, moving
them to different areas and varying them so much that the
horse thinks he's working something entirely new each day he's
brought up to it. The best way to set up a practice course is
to make one that is easily changeable with obstacles not too
heavy that they can't be moved. You'll need good, stout poles
(like telephone poles) for backthrough training, but you'll find

that even these can be rolled into a new position by two or three people.

RIDING OUTSIDE THE ARENA

There is NOTHING better for a trail horse than being ridden out on the trails or in the hills, where he can relax and enjoy himself and at the same time, be introduced to new things. A trail horse has to accept change. We find that horses who have been raised in box stalls or small corrals and "never been off the farm" don't accept change as readily as horses raised out in the open or ridden out a great deal. We also find horses that are ridden out tend to be less cranky than those constantly drilled in an arena. Stall-raised horses are often spooky and silly. The first thing we do with a horse like this is take him through the hill trails with a quiet pony horse. At first, the horse is scared of his own shadow, but later, because the pony horse is quiet, the stall-raised horse accepts the new surroundings. When he becomes confident, we start riding him with the same quiet pony horse brought along by another rider. When he is super-confident, he starts going out "solo," being ridden alone.

What changes take place? This horse will work obstacles better at home because he's learning to accept anything. He'll have a new confidence in what you put before him. He's less spooky. For example, with the pony horse, the "spook" is taken into a creek and allowed to stand and drink. Sometimes with stall-raised horses, it's a real event—because they're not used to water and they have no intentions of getting their feet wet! We take their water away for several hours, then take them up to the creek with a pony horse and let them drink. They find new joy in water because they're thirsty! Later, when being asked to work a water obstacle, the horse will be more likely to step right in. Without this basic outside riding, acceptance of a water box might not be so easy.

Not *all* stall-raised horses are "silly," but many lack confidence and are afraid to accept new things. Even if you have to trailer several miles to outside trails, it would be extremely beneficial to your trail-horse prospect. You can often find things such as natural logs to step your horse over, or to jump. So at the same time that you are relaxing the horse "outside," you'll be teaching him to work obstacles which he'll learn to readily accept.

Regardless of which phase of schooling you're working on, whether it be the basics, riding trails, or advanced schooling, *don't ever get mad at your horse!* If you try to discipline your horse while your temper is at its peak, you'll overdiscipline, or possibly give him "a little extra that he doesn't deserve." If you find yourself getting horribly upset, get off and try again another day. You have to look at both sides of the coin. Will it hurt the horse more to leave an obstacle he isn't working right, or will it hurt him more if you lose your temper and "beat the devil out of him" at the obstacle? Definitely, the latter. If you were being calm and collected, you could work with that horse until he *tried* to do the obstacle properly, but if you're about to blow your stack, it's better to quit. Get off and quit, or just ride the horse away from the obstacle and go out on the trail where you can both settle down.

You've undoubtedly, at horse shows, seen someone take a horse off in a corner and hit or spur him repeatedly. If it's a novice rider, you can bet a lot of the problem isn't with the horse, but rather with the rider's temper and his inability to control it. Many riders become embarrassed if their horses foul up in the show ring in front of their friends, so they take it out on the horse. This is one of my pet peeves, for I see it at each show I attend, more often than not with young riders who have no idea of the harm they're causing. The horses that "blow up" constantly on the trail course or during the rail work are usually the ones that have been knocked about by hot-tempered riders. It becomes a vicious circle. The horse blows up because he has been knocked on unnecessarily, so the rider keeps on, and the horse blows up again.

Trail-horse training takes PATIENCE. It also develops patience. There will be times when you should spend up to a half an hour just sitting on your horse, relaxing him at an obstacle. There will be times when you will be schooling on the L-shaped backthrough and will have ten minutes or so between each step the horse takes. This develops your patience and your horse's. It produces a horse who works his obstacles quietly and calmly and never rushes, and produces a rider that never expects too much of his horse. This is the type of training that takes a high-strung horse and gives you his MIND so he learns to settle down and become a trail horse. This is what takes the calm horse and KEEPS him that way. Whatever you do with your trail horse, THINK carefully about how it will affect him now, and in the future.

1.5. Remember, trail-horse training takes PATIENCE. A trail horse has to work the obstacles quietly and calmly. A good Western trail horse will never rush through the obstacles.

Chapter Two

What to Look For in a Trail Prospect

Trail classes, in the past, seemed to be a series of horrors. It was often one spooky obstacle after another. It's different now. Courses are being set up to test the agility of the trail horse and of his rider. To be successful, a trail horse has to have an overall agility and talent, and the rider has to know how to show it to the judge.

What does a trail horse need in addition to agility? In a prospect, temperament should be the first consideration. A trail horse has to be calm and willing. A kind horse with a good disposition just naturally stands a better chance of becoming a winner. Judges pay close attention to the attitude displayed by a trail horse, and if the horse is cranky and nasty, he won't score well.

A trail horse needs plenty of natural caution. He has to *want* to look at the obstacles and he needs to be the type of horse that checks things out, rather than just clumsily stumbling across them. A horse that walks over anything without showing any concern isn't going to be a consistent winner. A horse that takes a close look and investigates—one that is curious—has the edge.

This brings up the problem of extremely quiet, "sleepy"

15

2.1. *A trail-horse prospect needs plenty of natural caution. He has to WANT to look at the obstacles and he needs to be the type of horse that checks things out. A horse that takes a close look and investigates has the edge.*

horses. They can be clumsy and disinterested. People should be more concerned with finding a not-so-quiet horse rather than the quiet prospect that would walk off the edge of a cliff, if you aimed him in that direction!

If you've been out looking for a trail-horse prospect, and you've found a horse you think is a good one, test him. Set up a simple ground pole and lead the horse over. If he trips and hits the pole, wasn't looking, and showed no reaction to the fact that something touched his feet, he's sleepy and insensitive. If he takes a look at the pole and picks his feet up well to go over it, he's a better prospect. To take a look at the pole, a horse doesn't have to drop his head to the ground. A trail horse starts doing that later. A sensitive, cautious prospect, however, will look, even if just out of the corner of his eye, at that pole and "feel" with his feet to be sure he doesn't touch it.

Test the "spook control." Set up a few spooky things like a hide, or a plastic tarp hung on a fence. Lead him, or if he's broke, ride him, near these obstacles. Test him. If he pays no attention at all and walks by as if there's nothing there, I'd worry about making a good trail horse out of him. He's a little too quiet. If he takes a good look at these things and even spooks a little, you'll see how you can control him and if you can talk him into accepting your control. That's what you're after—a horse that looks because he's cautious—and one that will quickly calm down after he sees that nothing is going to hurt him. If he spooks wildly, blows up, and gives you the longest battle of your life, then he's no doubt one of those high-strung horses that takes a horribly long time to settle down. It's a task to teach such a horse.

There is a definite difference between natural caution and "head-for-the-hills-spook." It's natural for a trail horse to be a little afraid of things in the beginning, and if he is, you can use it to your advantage in producing a horse that really looks at his obstacles. You do it by instilling *confidence* in your trail horse. A silly, high-strung, and nervous horse just doesn't come around for you like the horse that has a lot of natural caution tied in with a good disposition. With a "good-minded" horse, you work to turn fear to acceptance. With a high-strung horse, you'll never know when he's going to let you down by blowing up over a simple obstacle. He'll never be the type of horse you can trust to be cool and calm. A horse like this generally wants to hurry over everything and get it over with fast. Hurrying is natural, even with the good prospect, but while you CAN slow the good prospect down through simple schooling, you run into a barrier with the nervous or bad-dispositioned horse. He might be working on a very simple task and get silly. He'll give you problems when you don't need them and don't want them. For example, we had a gelding who was a do-everything-fast, hyper kind of horse. For no apparent reason, he would

2.2. *The successful trail horse has to have both agility and talent and the rider has to know how to show it to the judge.*

have days when he was so "rotten," he wasn't fit to ride. These days were much too frequent. Like many nervous horses, he couldn't keep his mind on what he was doing. He'd blow up over the sight of something a block away when he was supposed to be looking at an obstacle. This horse was very representative of his pedigree, a strain known for hot, cranky, switchy dispositions. A horse like this will often begin bit chewing and gapping out of nerves, even when given nothing by the rider to make him nervous! Why spend an extra year trying to work out the problems of a "bad-minded," silly horse, when you could spend less time and have so much more enjoyment working on a nice prospect with a good mind?

WHAT ABOUT SIZE?

There are so many different calibers of trail courses. In the larger shows on the West Coast, most trainers seem to feel that an extremely tall horse or one a great deal smaller than the others is going to have major difficulty competing with the tough obstacles in today's big shows. Many obstacles are so tricky they require a horse to do some extremely "dressagey" movements and a horse that doesn't fit the space is handicapped. When you get down to the local show level, and many of the smaller breed shows, you won't be facing the type of obstacles that can foul up a horse if he's a little too tall or short.

Most of the trainers I talked to liked a "big show" horse to be in the range of 15 to 15.1 hands, but each had been successful with a smaller or larger horse, to a certain extent. The fact is clear that it's not so much what size a horse is, but whether or not he can USE his size and his body. Maybe a large horse will learn to travel more narrow and compensate for his size. A little horse might learn to reach if he has to and stretch to work something. Let's look at two "extremes."

Candy Bar, the white mare shown on page 23 is only about 14.1 and has competed successfully at large shows, such as the Junior Grand National at the Cow Palace. At local shows, she has earned enough ribbons to cover her owner's wall and fill several boxes. This mare is very agile and if she has to reach to step over an obstacle spaced for a larger horse, she strides boldly and does it.

A top trail-horse mare on the West Coast in former years was a big mare, standing 16.1. She was so agile, so well broke, and so talented, that she consistently won, no matter how tough the competition. On the "A" and "B" show circuit, she was often a show champion. Her trainer could do just about anything with her, and to prove her agility, could actually gather her up and turn her completely around on a VERY narrow bridge. This mare was short-coupled, which was much to her advantage, because an extremely tall, long-backed horse often brings problems. It's like parking a freight train in a Volkswagen space.

These two extremes are representative of horses that are away from the "norm" of trail horses, but were successful because of their agility and ability to USE their size. This certainly doesn't mean that horses the size of Candy, or of the larger mare, will be able to work like they did. These two are definitely athletes; not all horses are.

My philosophy is simply to DO THE BEST WITH WHAT YOU HAVE. If you're not planning on showing in the biggest and toughest shows, then you can get by and win at the local level with a horse that is just NOT the "size accepted by top professionals." We, as backyard horsemen, find ourselves getting horribly attached to our horses. While a trainer is busy with a full barn of horses to school, we don't find ourselves in that circumstance. One or two horses seem to take up our time, and because we want to work with them, we would certainly not sell them because they didn't fit the specifications of exactly what a "top" horse should be.

There is such an incredible difference between the smaller and larger shows and the trail courses they set up. If you enjoy the small, local shows, the 4-H sponsored shows, or the breed shows in your area that are fairly small and nice to attend, then you don't NEED a horse that can win at the Cow Palace or take home a state championship. I show because I love it. I love the competition, the chance to be around people I like, and the challenge of it all. I find a great deal of satisfaction in being stubborn and taking a horse that someone might have laughed at, and making him into a winner. There is a great deal of controversy in the horse world. A person who likes halter horses will tell you to sell your trail horse if he doesn't have a big long hip! A person who likes the classy, open Western pleasure horse will judge all horses by this type, regardless of what they're cut out to do. You have to find what YOU like and go with it.

A trail horse just doesn't need to be horribly expensive. Naturally, he'll be worth a lot when he's well schooled, but many of the horses showing today, even the TOP ones, weren't bred and raised to become show champions. They just "happened." Certainly the beauty of the trail horse is that so many are "Cinderella horses."

Not too many years ago, a Pacific Coast champion trail horse for the "A" circuit was an unregistered, chestnut mare. She traveled to the major open shows in quest of her title, and few horses ever topped her performances. She won show championships at many of the toughest open shows on the West Coast.

At the first Grand Prix for trail horses held at San Francisco's Cow Palace, the Cinderella theme prevailed. One of the finalists, competing for over $2,000 in prize money, was a former pack horse, who had spent years traveling the mountain trails with a string of mules. Another top competitor was a cute Paint mare that cost her owner about $200. Realizing the potential, the owner studied under a top trail-horse trainer. The mare now competes with the best trail horses on the coast, and she's in the ribbons more often than not. Still another Grand Prix contestant was a former bucking horse. Another was a ranch horse who was used in the winter to drag bales of hay through the mud with a lariat, to assist in feeding a herd of hungry cattle. These are just some of the horses that have become consistent winners because someone took the time to notice their potential and took the effort to school them.

Some people feel it takes years to make a top-rate trail horse. You may be showing your horse in a matter of weeks, if you go to schooling shows with very basic courses, but the fact is, it's going to take you a long time to teach your horse "everything." There are no shortcuts. You're after CONFIDENCE, and trust in your horse. You get this from proper schooling. If you hurt a horse, he won't work for you.

I've seen some pretty strange methods used in the rush to produce an instant winner. I've seen BB guns turned down low and aimed at the legs of a horse who was shot in the fetlock area each time he didn't raise his feet high enough when going over poles. I've seen people "behind the barn," before a class, poling a horse on stepovers. This is done by taking a horse over a pole which two people are holding. As the horse goes over, the pole is raised and banged against the horse's feet or legs. Since he becomes afraid of getting hurt, he raises his feet. What happens when he goes into the class and the people aren't there holding the pole? Chances are, he'll stumble over it. If a horse is so clumsy and lacks the agility to step clearly over a simple pole, then hurting him or scaring him isn't going to give him any agility—it's going to make him mad, cranky, and resentful. Maybe there are some "pro" trainers who have gimmicky methods they use in tuning up an old horse who has become sloppy. But, unlike a novice, when they're using a method, they know how to do it to benefit. Personally, I don't believe in BB guns or poling, tack boards, or forcing a horse. This is all part of trying to make something out of a horse who is not capable of doing the job. Have you ever seen a rider in a "fight" with a horse, spurring and hitting it to get up to a gate? It's a lot easier to start with the very basics, and keep the horse quiet! If he knows all the basic moves BEFORE he's ever

2.3. Patience and understanding produce confidence in any horse that is being trained—and confidence is what makes a trail-horse prospect a winner.

brought up to a gate, and if he's introduced to a gate as a thing to relax around, he'll be GOOD at gates.

Gimmicks and shortcuts and temper losses don't train trail horses. Patience and understanding are what produce confidence, and confidence is what makes a winner. Show him what you want. Don't force him into something when he has no idea what he's supposed to do.

At the same time you're working on schooling your horse, particularly on relaxation and concentration, you have to work on it yourself! The biggest problem with a novice learning to ride trail horses in the show ring is to learn to look at each obstacle BEFORE going into the ring and to plan a strategy. It's not an overnight thing. In the beginning, you might plot it all outside of the course, then get a bad case of nerves when you ride through the gate. Work to change this. Think about all you've practiced at home. Know before you enter the ring exactly how you'll approach and work each obstacle. You have to THINK out each obstacle as you come to it and keep your plan going. As soon as you finish one obstacle, turn and go on to the next one, giving your entire concentration to what you'll do next.

In a pleasure class, you can get away with blocking things out. You can go around on the rail, just keeping a good spot, and not have to worry about much else. A trail class is tough, however, because you have to think and plan. Its like a reining-horse class.

Before a reining-horse rider enters the ring, he knows where he's going to make his run down and stop. He checks ground conditions. If all the other horses before him have run and stopped on the same line of ground, it's going to be torn up. The next rider might feel he'll get a better run down and stop a few feet off from that line. He chooses his place to run, and his place to stop. What if he didn't plan the stop? There he'd be, running wide open down the arena and all of a sudden going into a panic, snatching his horse's head and getting an untimed, unbalanced stop. Compare this to a trail class. If you don't PLAN and you don't THINK, you can't WIN!

Many novice riders, in the beginning, get so upset over not working one obstacle cleanly, that it causes them to lose their concentration throughout the rest of the course. If you make a mistake, that certainly doesn't mean you won't be in the ribbons. Wipe it out of your mind completely and concentrate on the rest of the course. *Remember, a winner thinks about what strategy he'll use to do things right. A loser worries about what can go wrong.*

Chapter Three

Basic Training for the Western Trail Horse

When you get right down to the facts about today's trail classes, you can plainly see that they've changed since their original formation. It's no longer a case of working simple obstacles that are much like you'd find out on the trail. Today there are many dressage-type obstacles—difficult ones, requiring the highest degree of body control. Most require a horse to do a sidepass, turn on the forehand, turn on the haunches, and careful backing. Many are a combination of all of these movements. You can't just ride a horse up to an obstacle such as a gate or an L-shaped backthrough and expect him to work it without any former training or body control. If you DO give him the basics and teach him these movements, there's no reason why you shouldn't be able to work ANY obstacle fairly well the first time you try it.

All the basics should be taught AWAY from the obstacles, in an arena, open field, or schooling pen. Your horse will learn to respond to your cues and become *confident* in these movements. When he has them down to a science and you take him to a difficult body-control-type obstacle, he shouldn't have to worry about what to do—he'll know from your cues. Let's look at what happens if you teach the basics wrong at an obstacle.

Have you ever seen anyone straddling a horse over a log or pole and yanking at his head and spurring him to sidepass? The horse has NO idea of what he's supposed to do. Added to the confusion is possible injury. If the horse moves up, the disgusted rider will snatch the reins and hurt a tender mouth. As the horse moves, he hits his legs on logs or poles. That hurts! If he moves his hindquarters in the wrong direction, he gets a jab with the rider's heels. It all ends in a blow up and the chance the horse will never sidepass at all because he's so upset over it!

What if this horse was taught to sidepass and the rider could position him and move him easily and quietly? He could then ride the horse up, position the log or pole properly under the center of the horse, then cue him to sidepass. The horse would KNOW what was being asked and would sidepass over calmly, probably paying little or no attention to the log. Since the rider had body control on this horse, he could keep him positioned so the horse's legs would never touch the pole. This builds confidence! The obstacle hasn't hurt the horse and the horse is doing "something old" that he knows well. Give YOUR trail horse that chance! Teach him all of these basics:

1. To move away from leg pressure.
2. To turn on the forehand.
3. To turn on the haunches.
4. To sidepass.
5. To move any single foot into any position through reining.
6. To respect the word "WHOA" and know that it means STOP, and not slow down.
7. To back easily either on voice or very slight rein pressure—or better yet, *both* ways.

MOVING AWAY FROM PRESSURE

A horse's natural instinct is to move *against* pressure. How many times have you tried to move a horse over while brushing him, only to have him push right back against you? It's a natural reaction, but it's one that you change through schooling, for a horse must learn to GIVE to pressure and move away from it.

You can start this schooling with a very young horse, or you can wait until you're ready to start serious schooling with a broke horse you're ready to make a trail horse out of. Whenever you get the chance, hold the horse's head and, with your fingers, push against his sides near where your heel or calf would be if you were in the saddle. If he takes a step or two *away* from your hand, praise him and quit at that. Ask him

3.1. A horse must learn to give to pressure and to move away from it. Start his training from the ground. Hold your horse's head and with your fingers, push against his sides near where your heel or calf would be if you were in the saddle. If he takes a step or two away from your hand, praise him and quit at that.

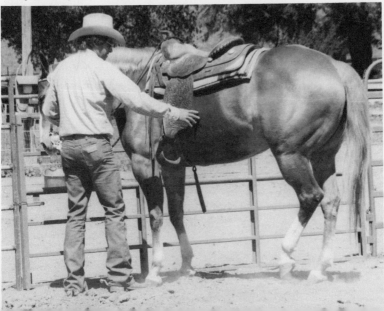

for an extra step the next time. If he *doesn't* move away, but moves into the pressure, get a spur or a stick—something he'll feel more readily—and press that against his sides, releasing the pressure the *instant* he takes a step in the right direction.

You should do this from the ground often, until you can hold a horse's head and move his hindquarters away from you in an 180-degree turn. Then, start it from the saddle. Steady his head, leg him and push him over, away from your leg pressure. Not too much at once, now! If you get a step or two the first few tries, put him away happy. If you try to get too much out of him too soon, he won't understand it and he'll get angry. He'll rightly "lock up" on you because he's not sure what you want.

Turn on the Forehand

Where do you use a turn on the forehand in a trail course? There are many instances. You do a quarter-turn while working a gate. You do this when your horse reaches the turning point in the L-shaped backthrough and must hold his front feet steady while swinging his hindquarters around into a turn. A pivot in a tire with the front feet in the tire center is a turn on the forehand. To keep from getting mixed up, remember that a turn on the forehand is just that—the horse is rotating off his front end while his back end moves around it in a pivot. The turn on the haunches is the opposite. The haunches remain stationery and the front end rotates around.

If you taught your horse to move away from leg pressure, this should be a cinch to teach! You can either try it from the ground first, or from the saddle. Place his head into a fence corner or rail when working from the ground. This will keep his front end from moving forward out of position. Steady his head and push against his sides until he moves away from the pressure. That's the beginning. When he gets the idea, climb aboard and position his head into the corner of the fence. If

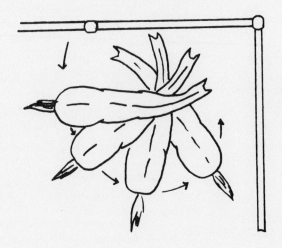

3.A. A turn on the forehand is when the horse is rotating off his front end while his back end moves around it in a pivot.

you use a snaffle bit, keep your hands wide and low to steady his head. If you use a regular bridle, position your hand above the horse and keep his body fairly straight. You may have to bend his head a little at first into the *opposite* direction as you're asking his hindquarters to move, but as soon as he gets the idea, try to keep his body fairly straight.

A trail horse must be taught to move slowly and carefully. One way to instill this in him is to ask for one step at a time when doing the turn on the forehand. Hold him with your hands, move him one step with your leg, then stop. Move him another step, then stop. If he's taught to do it slowly, he'll eventually be taken to an obstacle to do this movement. He'll work the obstacle slowly, because he knows that's the way he's to do the turn on the forehand—carefully and without hurry.

Don't try to do a turn on the forehand away from the fence

3.2. *The* V-*shaped sidepass obstacle involves a turn on the forehand. Lew negotiates it with Flaxie.*

3.3. *The horse sidepasses to the* V *and her front legs remain in place while her hind end is brought around to the right. The horse will then continue to sidepass off the obstacle.*

until the horse is acting like he understands it completely. The fence is a crutch for him at first and if you take him out in the open too soon and try the turn, he may try to get out of the situation by moving forward.

To get a better idea of what you're trying to teach the horse, look at the two photos of Lew Silva working Flaxie on a V-shaped sidepass. Flaxie is sidepassed to the V center. Her front legs then remain set and Lew legs the mare's back end around for a turn on the forehand. Then, he sidepasses off. This simple obstacle is one of many that requires this movement. Since the mare has been schooled thoroughly on this movement AWAY from the obstacles, she knows that movement well enough to know she must not move forward. If she did move, she'd hit and roll the poles with her back feet.

TURN ON THE HAUNCHES

This movement is a little more confusing for a horse and a little harder to teach. It is, however, very essential, so take the time to get it clear in the horse's mind. It's probably best to master the turn on the forehand first, then work on this. Trying to teach both at once might confuse a green trail horse.

In this turn on the haunches the horse is pivoting or "working off" his hind end. His body is moved around so that his front end makes a big circle and his back legs shift just a little to make a very small circle. The hind legs stay in almost the same place moving only in a pivot-type movement without backing up or going forward.

Again, you can use a corner or straight rail to advantage to help contain the horse. His first defense will be to back up and you have to discourage this. If you use a corner and back him in so that one side of the rail is parallel to his body and the other rail is right behind him, you can contain him easier. Even the straight rail works but a corner might work even better. If you're using a corner with a fence alongside, you can take him from that fence in a turn on the haunches until the fence which was behind him is then parallel to the other side of his body. That gives you a half-turn. You can then reverse the movement and go back to the original position and you've done a turn in the other direction.

This turn is similar to the motion in opening and closing a gate. The horse's back legs act as the "hinge" and the "gate," or his body, swing around.

If you're positioned in the corner so the fence is behind your horse and the other rail is at your left leg parallel to the horse, you can begin teaching him to do a turn on the haunches to the right. Start by positioning yourself correctly. Sit way back

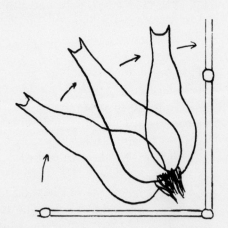

3.B. A turn on the haunches.

and down in the saddle. This anchors the horse's hindquarters, making it harder for him to move them. If you mistakingly get up out of the saddle and lean forward, it's an open invitation for the horse to walk forward right out of the corner. Sit down deep in the saddle and gather the horse between your hands and legs.

Lew is using a regular bridle (with a curb bit) in the photos on page 34, so he is simply reining the mare's front end around while the back end remains steady. He's also using his legs. The best way to describe the movement and rider aids is to tell how it's done with two hands on the reins when a snaffle bit is used. In moving to the right, your right hand would be "pulling" and the left hand would be steadying and keeping the horse from overbending. Your right hand holds the direct rein which is moved out to lead the horse's head *slightly* into the direction he is to turn. Your right leg will be just about at the girth, applying just enough pressure to limit the movements of the quarters and to maintain the impulsion.

The left aids are different. Your outside leg will be about six inches *behind* the girth, to discourage the horse from swinging his rear end out to the left and moving out of pivot position. Your left hand is used for an indirect rein, held low in front of the wither area. This acts to draw the horse back, rocking him back on his haunches while he moves to the right with his front end. Like the turn on the forehand, you ask for a movement ONE STEP AT A TIME. With the first few sessions, you might only ask for a step or two, then quit. As the horse progresses, you do the "step-stop-step" schooling to keep him moving slowly and carefully. As he progresses even more, you can put him back into his regular bridle, as Lew has done in the photos with Flaxie on page 36, place him out of the corner, backed into a rail, and just rein his front end around, trying to keep his body straight. Don't try teaching him to do this away from the fence until you're sure he understands it.

A turn on the haunches is like the "spin" or offset turn done by a stock horse. The body remains relatively straight and the horse rocks back on his hindquarters, plants an inside, or pivot foot, and swings his front end around for the spin. A well-trained trail horse is doing essentially the same thing with a turn on the haunches. If he's the type of horse you can "wake up," you should someday be able to start the turn on the

3.4. *The V-shaped sidepass obstacle can also involve a turn on the haunches.*

3.5. *The horse sidepasses to the V and her hind legs remain in place while her front end is brought around the point. The horse will then continue to sidepass off the obstacle.*

haunches, cluck at him to speed him up, and actually get a spin out of him.

Let's look at the concept slowly, "trail-horse style." Check the second set of photos of Lew working the V-shaped sidepass on page 34. The horse's forequarters are toward you. Flaxie is being sidepassed toward the right to the V where her hind legs will remain in place while her front end is brought around. In the second photo, Flaxie is doing this turn on the haunches and will then continue to sidepass off the obstacle.

SIDEPASSING

Many people fail to realize just how hard it is for a horse to understand what a sidepass is! It's natural for him to move forward or back, but not sideways! You have to be extremely patient with this schooling, and no matter how slow you go, you can expect the horse to get a little frustrated and mad until he gets the idea completely and learns to handle himself.

There are two basic methods we use in teaching sidepassing. The first is one which makes a horse less angry. Look at the diagram on sidepassing on page 37, as well as the two photos on page 36 which show Lew Silva walking Flaxie in a circle. He is holding the reins in both hands, which can be done with either a regular bridle or a snaffle. As he circles to the left, he is bending the horse into the direction of the circle with light inside rein, and pushing the hindquarters AWAY from the circle with his left leg. With this type of schooling, your leg pressure is light until you've completed one or two circles. Then, as shown in the diagram, you begin pushing the horse out AWAY from the circle. This is done by using stronger leg pressure pushing the horse out from the center of the circle, and direct reining, or neckreining the horse into the same direction. When you get even a step or two "out of the circle," you've started a sidepass, and you should stop and pet the horse and praise him for it. Release

3.6, 3.7. One way to teach a horse to sidepass is schooling in a circle as shown here. The horse has to be able to respond to leg pressure.

3.C. To teach sidepassing, start by circling.

all leg and rein pressure and let him stand. Next lesson, ask for another step or two and GRADUALLY increase it until he's sidepassing well. Remember that, in the beginning, it's much easier to teach him after he's moving in the circle. Trying it from a dead standstill might confuse him.

If the circling method doesn't work, you can walk him up to a fence and let him face it. Keep him moving quietly. As the head faces the fence, rein his front end to the right for just ONE step, then push with your left leg to move his hindquarters to the right. What you're doing is breaking the sidepass up into two parts. First, the front end moves, then the hindquarters "catch up." Stop and praise him, let him stand for a moment, then ask for a second set of steps and QUIT. Next lesson, increase it by a step or two and GRADUALLY increase it, working up until you're asking for BOTH the front and back ends to move together. Always do this SLOWLY with pauses after every couple of steps. Many horses don't like to sidepass and want to do it quickly. This should be halted, or you'll develop a bad habit that will lose you a lot of classes when you later ask the horse to sidepass an obstacle and he "runs off" it sideways. Remember, a good trail horse is *careful*, picking his way over and through everything.

Moving One Foot at a Time

If you were in an L-shaped backthrough, to cite an example, and your horse was standing with his left foot straddled out to the side too close to the pole, you'd want to move that foot back into proper position but you would NOT want to have to swing the entire front end over to do it. By very light, very intricate movement, you should be able to rein the horse "just enough" that he'd move that foot a little to the right. This type of slight position change might get you out of a lot of trouble in many types of obstacles, so you must practice it AWAY from the obstacles. Many riders overdo cues and get too much movement. You have to learn to use "just a little" cue to get the job done.

Let's say you have a regular bridle on your horse and you want to move his left front leg over to the left. VERY lightly rein him until he moves it a little to the left. Don't leg him, as it might cause him to move his entire body or move the wrong leg. All you want is that one foot to move slightly, and the body to stay where it is. When you've moved the foot a little to the left, try reining it back a little to the right. Work with each front foot until you feel you can place a foot anywhere you want it.

"Whoa"

If a horse responds to the word "whoa" you can make a much smoother trip through a trail course. If a judge sees you stop your horse without having to "haul him back" and restrain him heavily, you're going to score more points. When you use a voice command in a show ring, you only have to "whisper" it so the horse hears—not the crowd. You start at home with very firm schooling on stopping and standing.

Put a halter on your horse and use a chain or other type of shank that you can run through under his chin. Walk him along, then say "whoa" as you take hold of the shank and stop him. Repeat this over several sessions until the horse is stopping on voice more than pull. Be sure you NEVER allow him to move or try and wander off until YOU want him to move. If he starts to move on his own, tell him "WHOA" again and hold him with the shank. Begin teaching him from the saddle, taking hold of his head and saying "whoa," working until he's stopping from a walk or jog on the voice command more so than the reins. Make him STAND still until you're ready for him to move. What you're trying to do is freeze him in a position. Many riders use the word "whoa" too casually, saying it when they only want a horse to slow down. Then the horse doesn't accept it as being the word to "freeze" his movement. Use it only to STOP and hold the horse. Many top trail horses are so well schooled on the word that they will freeze at any time. If they're working stepovers and a foot is up and the rider says "whoa," they'll stop with that foot off the ground.

BACKING

This is such a big part of trail schooling! A trail horse MUST give his head and back lightly. A lot of bitting-up helps a great deal. Ground-driving to stop and back a horse is another way to get him to give his head and back readily. Probably the easiest way to get a horse to give and *come back to you* is to stop him by merely steadying your hands—NOT pulling back. If you're using a snaffle, place your hands low and steady and HOLD them there. Don't pull back. As you hold your hands still with some rein tension, use equal leg pressure on each side, and use the word "back" or cluck to the horse. He'll try to push out against your hands at first, but your hands will remain steady. He can't go forward, and he feels the leg pressure and knows he has to go *somewhere*, so he'll "give to your hands and come back to you." As he steps back and nods his head back to you, release the hand and leg pressure instantly and pet him. Try it again. This is something to do often while teaching a horse to give to bridle pressure. When he's giving well, you can put him in his regular bridle and hold your hand steady as you leg him, possibly coaxing him just a little with a slight movement of your hand, clucking him or giving the word "back" for each *careful* step you want. You should be able to back him almost totally on that word command in case you get in a pinch at an obstacle and want to bring him back just a step or two without touching his head.

Remember that a judge is looking for any move you might make that shows your horse is NOT broke properly, such as having to pull extremely hard to back the horse. He wants to see the horse move back WITHOUT seeing you make him do it. You should teach your horse to back ever so lightly on voice and rein and he should stop backing when you release leg pressure or tell him "whoa."

Without teaching a horse all these basics, you just can't take him to a trail course and expect him to work the body-control-type obstacles successfully. If you DO take the time to school him on these movements before taking him on obstacles, you should be able to work almost anything the first time you try it, whether it be a pivot in a tire, a gate, an L-shaped backthrough, or a sidepass. Give your horse a chance!

Chapter Four

Setting Up a Practice Trail Course

There's something about training a trail horse that brings out the scavenger in a person! You'll find junk yards and wood piles exciting places to go to when you're out to "scrounge." One man's junk is another man's treasure, and this is surely true when you're out looking for items to help set up your trail course.

You'll find in this book many suggestions about types, weights, and sizes of materials and how to use them in your horse's training. The chapters on different obstacles will clue you in on spacing, variation, and schooling. *This* chapter will give you ideas about important items needed for your own basic trail course. Variations of basic obstacles will be shown. You can vary any obstacle, if you just put on your thinking cap, and it is SO important to vary them! Never drill a horse over and over on the same obstacle or you'll produce a horse that only does it out of *habit*. If you have a permanent L-shaped backthrough set up, and you work the horse on it day after day, turning to the left in the corner and backing out, he'll give you a battle when you someday try and work it in another direction. He'll get sloppy in his footwork because he's bored from doing it the same way over and over. Try to

4.1. Wendy's railed bridge has "walk-up" ramps on each end.

4.2. This higher railless bridge can be used with no "extras" for the fairly green horse.

set up obstacles that you can constantly change, constantly move, and even stick in a corner out of the way, if you feel your horse has seen enough of it for awhile.

If we recommend that an obstacle should be heavy and immovable, then make it heavy enough so the horse can't roll it if he hits it. This doesn't mean that it should be so grossly heavy that YOU can never move it. Keep everything as portable as possible!

BRIDGES

When you first start your horse on bridges, you'll start him on something low, naturally solid and wide enough that he's not likely to slip off the edge. As he progresses, you can change it.

By taking a flat object, such as a *heavy* sheet of plywood, and laying it on the ground, you can introduce your horse to the concept of a bridge. Later, he'll be ready for something such as the white, railed bridge in the top photograph on page 42, which Wendy Daniels uses to school Candy Bar on. It is wide enough so the rider doesn't get hung up going through, if the horse doesn't travel exactly down the middle. You can see the ramp-type edge on the openings of the bridge, a type often found in show rings. This is more of a "walk-up" than a step-up bridge. It can easily be varied by placing some sort of metal pole under the center to make it a teetering bridge.

When a horse is farther along, he can be schooled on a higher, more narrow bridge without rails. Barbara is holding Dusty on such a bridge which is beneficial in schooling horses to step on and off with some "grace." At first, their efforts are somewhat clumsy. Later, they get coordinated.

This high, step-up bridge can be varied for a more finished horse. In the photos on page 44, a variation is shown, using tires. There is one set flush up against the "on" side of the bridge, and one on the step-down side. Barbara, riding Good

4.3. By placing a tire before and after the bridge, Barbara has made it a little tougher and more challenging for this finished trail-horse mare.

4.4. The big step down requires a foot to go right in the center of the tire.

News up, lets the mare drop her head and investigate. The mare steps in the tire, goes over the bridge, and steps dead center in the tire center coming down. To make this much more difficult, a tire can be placed *on* the bridge, giving the horse a total of three tires to work with the bridge.

If you're working on learning how to keep a horse on a narrow bridge, you can make one by using a long, narrow sheet of heavy wood, strong enough to take the weight of your horse. Heavy plywood about six feet long by two or two and one-half feet wide will keep you on your toes, especially if you elevate just *one* end by placing a tire under it.

What else can you do with a bridge? You can lay cuttings of weeds or bushes across it, set down a tarp or hide, place a stepover pole just in front of the bridge, or at the point where the horse steps off, or on the bridge itself. Old coats made of fuzzy material make fake hides that you can lay across a bridge. (See Chapter 10 for more ideas.)

STEPOVERS

Get out your empty paint cans, railroad ties, pipes—anything you can think of to step your horse over. Go out to an orchard or any place where you can pick up some natural logs. Find some railroad ties, some old telephone poles or jump poles. Those jump poles can be easily made by taking a 4×4 and shaving off each of the four edges, making each edge flat. You can then paint them with stripes, using different colors so each one draws the "individual" attention of the horse. It wouldn't hurt to have more than a dozen of these poles.

Jump poles can be placed in a variety of ways to teach a horse to become clever on stepovers. Chapter 6 will tell you about spacing and when to work the horse on "tough" spacing. You can use the type of pole that Wendy is walking Candy Bar over (see p. 46), and elevate each pole end with a paint can. Laying poles under the ends, parallel to Candy, would

4.5. Regular jump poles can be used as stepovers.

also elevate the stepover. You can often alternate. In this four-pole stepover, for instance, the first and third pole could be elevated on the left sides only, the second and forth pole on the right sides only. If you want to make it a little spooky, place a tarp or some foil under it.

In the top photo on page 47, Barbara is leading Dusty over a single natural log. It's wide enough so that he's not tempted to step out and solid enough so that he can feel it hold its place if he touches it. It's also a good starter log because it's not so high and difficult that it would scare a green horse. Having several such logs scattered around your course as single obstacles would be beneficial.

Horses ready to start a series can be worked on a row of three or four logs. The first three in this series are smooth, cut poles. The fourth is a crooked natural log. This gets the

4.6. Single logs are good for starting green horses on stepovers.

4.7. This series is made up of three smooth round logs and a crooked natural log.

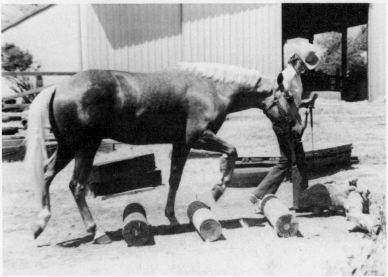

horse's attention because it's something different. How do you space them? For a green horse, you'd want to see where he would naturally step, and place them so that he can easily maneuver them. Later, you'll be scattering them and varying distance, to make him clever.

Stepover "traps" are often used to sharpen up finished horses that become somewhat lazy and aren't picking their feet up as well. The trap shown just below is made of two-inch pipe. If you held it up, it would look like a ladder. It is welded together to make it solid. This one has been varied

4.8. *Stepover "traps" can be made to sharpen up a horse on step-over obstacles.*

by setting it up on tires, and by tightly wiring two wooden logs over two of the pipes. This variation will make a horse pay close attention and really look at the obstacle. Traps can also be made by nailing together a series of 4×4s, using the same outer bracing as shown with the pipe trap.

One way to teach a horse to "look" at his obstacle is to get him to *smell* it. If you have certain materials on hand, you can vary each stepover pole so it smells a little different. The horse will begin searching and smelling each individual pole. Try "painting" the center of the poles with such things as corn oil, hoof dressing, fly spray, molasses, and corn syrup. Each pole should be painted with something a little different.

TIRES

Believe it or not, some of the service stations that give you credit on used tires when you buy new ones have to PAY to have the old ones hauled away. If they're not fit to become recaps, they congregate in a pile, and the station pays a flat fee for each tire that goes to the dump. Most of the time, if you drive into a service station and ask for old tires, you'll be greeted with a smile! A dozen car tires would be a good start. Finding larger tires is sometimes a little difficult, but certainly not impossible. You'll need low, tractor-type tires with big centers, and some larger tractor tires. Try finding some type of construction yard, or your town's maintenance crew vehicle yard. Anywhere there is a variety of tractors or trucks, there is a variety of tires ready for the graveyard. Reincarnate them. Take them home to your trail course.

Tires can be piled up to make jumps, used as walkthroughs, placed in water boxes and on bridges—you'll find many different uses for them in this book.

JUMPS

When you first start jumping your horse, you won't have a

4.9. *A row of tires is a common obstacle in the show ring. Tires are easily obtainable and should be used in home-schooling.*

4.10. Wendy uses a box designed to hold four tires. It can be filled with water to make it a tougher obstacle.

4.11. A low tire with a large center is the best type for use in schooling a green horse.

4.12. *Take advantage of outside obstacles for use as jumps, such as this log Good News is being taken over.*

lot of height for him to clear, but you WILL have to use solid objects so he won't learn that hitting them will knock them down. Telephone poles, railroad ties which can be stacked two-high, and natural logs all make good jumps. Taking advantage of natural logs out on the trail, to use when schooling over jumps, will help keep the horse "sharp" and interested.

Later, when the horse is well versed on jumps, you can use the light poles such as those used by Wendy Daniels when she schools Candy Bar. If you look closely at the photo on page 54, you can see the small standards. They are made with short pieces of 4×4 posts. On the side Candy faced before the jump, they are "step-like," made in a terraced way to use by simply laying the pole on. Regular jump standards can also be made.

What else can you jump? You can put two bales of hay end to end. Make a stack of tires, or a pile of firewood. When you're jumping your horse on spreads to get him to tuck and work more on his style, you can set a jump up with barrels laid down on their sides. Lay a row of three end-to-end barrels, then elevate a couple of railroad ties parallel in front of the barrels, or, if your horse is capable, another row of three barrels.

Vary your jumps by laying hides, tarps, or brush over them.

BACKTHROUGHS

When starting a green horse on backthroughs, you should never use light poles. In order to get the horse to use himself carefully and respect the backthroughs, you must use something heavy, such as railroad ties, or telephone poles. If he hits the obstacle with his feet, he'll quickly realize that he can't roll it away and he'll be more careful. When he's more finished, you'll go on to the type of poles shown in the photo on page 54 of the L-shaped backthrough.

4.13. *More finished horses can be schooled on lighter weight poles than those used to school a green horse.*

4.14. *Jump poles are laid down to form an L-shaped backthrough. Small poles such as these are used for working finished horses. Green horses should be schooled with railroad ties or telephone poles.*

To give you an idea of backthroughs and how one obstacle can be varied, there is a series of photos of a backthrough set up by Jim Crider beginning on page 56. Barbara Davison is working the Pinto mare. The backthrough is made of railroad ties and posts, with the smaller boards nailed to the ties so nothing can be knocked over. It is a two-cornered backthrough. The first photo shows the two corners. Barbara uses it as a regular backthrough by bringing the mare in, making one turn to the left as she would in an L-shaped backthrough, then still *another* left turn, then backs out. It can be entered from either side, so the horse can be schooled on left or right turns. A horse can be stepped in from the side and ridden to the point where he is facing the upper left corner, then backed and asked to do one turn and a back out. If the horse is brought in as Barbara is doing in the first photo, it can be backed around the first corner, then ridden forward and stepped out. Each time this obstacle is used, it can be varied.

4.15. This is a two-sided backthrough made up of posts and railroad ties which have been nailed in place to make it solid.

Can you see now, how you can take one simple obstacle and use it several different ways? Look at the additional possibilities:

By placing a plastic tub next to one of the edges, the backthrough becomes a STEPOVER AND WATER OBSTACLE. To make it even more difficult, two tires have been placed in front of the water tub, so the horse steps into each of the two tires, into the water box, and over two railroad ties.

This same obstacle could be sidepassed by going around the outer edge. A bridge-type board could be laid where the tires and box are set so that it raises from the ground to the top of the railroad tie. The horse would have to walk up on the ramp-type bridge, step down off the edge and over the second tie.

4.16, 17, 18. It can be used as a regular backthrough . . . and . . .

4.19. Add a plastic tub full of water and you have a combination stepover and water obstacle.

4.20. Add two tires and you have a more difficult obstacle.

Backarounds

Many shows ask a rider to back a horse around cloverleaf barrels. A set of three barrels is quite an asset to a practice course. When you first start schooling your horse, you'll ride him up to a *single* barrel and stand him there while you rock it with your foot. Your horse must get used to the barrel and not be afraid of the sound of your foot rubbing against it. You'll want to school him to stand quietly and accept it if

4.21. Try and acquire three barrels to school on backing through the cloverleaf pattern.

you push a barrel over with your foot. Many horses think if an obstacle falls down, they're going to get in deep trouble. Let him know that's not so. Work him on a single barrel first, and read Chapter 8 on backthroughs and backarounds to learn how to be ready to work the cloverleaf.

You may be asked to back around the same type of poles in the show ring, as pole benders use in timed events. They're an easy obstacle to make. Fill an empty paint can with cement and place a small pole in it. Make three or four of them for your practice course.

SIDEPASS OBSTACLES

Sidepass obstacles will vary from telephone poles and railroad ties, to bales of hay, barrels, and the regular "jump poles" shown in the photo of Wendy sidepassing Candy Bar on a simple V-shaped sidepass just below. Sidepassing is often made more difficult in the show ring by the tricky elevation of the poles. If you have several paint cans at home, you can use a couple of them to elevate your poles during schooling. You can also set up a sidepass pole on tires, or bales of hay, one bale on each end. This would require the bale to be turned

4.22. These poles have been set up for use as a sidepass obstacle.

over on it's side so it wouldn't be so high and difficult that you'd have to ride up and step the horse over the pole to get into sidepass position if the bale wasn't in a position that it, too, could be sidepassed. You can often use your backthroughs as sidepass obstacles, such as going around the outside poles of an L. See chapter 8 on sidepassing for more ideas.

WATER OBSTACLES

Never pass up a chance to ride a horse outside the arena, through streams and creeks, or even mud puddles. It will give a horse confidence when it comes to stepping in water. To make a natural type of water obstacle at home, you can simply dig a wide, long hole, lay a plastic tarp in it, and cover the tarp with a little dirt to keep it in place. This will keep the water *above* the ground, instead of under it. To make this obstacle even more interesting, build a small hill that the horse can come down off right into the water. You might be lucky to find workers digging a hole for someone's swimming pool. They're usually happy to have a place to dump the dirt and will often come right to your practice course and give you a load or two of dirt for your "mock hill." Don't be afraid to ask—that's how you acquire things!

Water boxes are easily constructed. Look at the one Wendy uses to school Candy Bar on page 64. It is a simple box lined with a heavy black plastic tarp to keep the water in. A little sand has been put on the bottom to keep it from being too slippery. This water box can easily be varied. In the next photo, Wendy has placed a stepover pole across the box and scattered brush around the front and sides. A tire could be

4.23. Riding "out" in creeks and streams, even mud puddles, can help your horse in his water-obstacle schooling. Quite often, a show-ring course is set up around natural obstacles, such as a creek.

4.24. Wendy uses a simple tarp-lined water box in her schooling.

4.25. *Here, it has been varied by adding a pole and laying some brush around the sides and front.*

placed in or before and after the box. Dry ice could be put into it to give the appearance of smoke. Throwing in a little laundry detergent and turning on a high-pressure hose sprayer would make mounds of bubbles. Pieces of wadded-up aluminum foil would make "strange floating things" on the surface of the water box.

Wendy also has a "tire box," shown on page 51, that is lined with a plastic tarp and can be easily filled for use as a "tricky" water box. What else can you use? Children's plastic wading pools make excellent water obstacles. If you can elevate four poles to form a big square, drop a tarp in the center and over the four edges and fill it up so it forms a small water obstacle. The water will stay mostly in the center. The horse will have to step over the elevated, tarp-covered pole, into the water, and then over another pole to get out.

WHAT ELSE?

Fill a gunny sack with old tin cans and tightly secure the ends. Many courses include an obstacle where a rider must pick up a sack of cans while mounted and carry them to a barrel or other obstacle and set them down. Some require you to mount the horse while holding the sack of cans. Use the sack in many ways to get the horse used to it.

A plain plastic bucket is good to have on your trail course. Practice filling it with water and carrying it while mounted from one place to another. Learn to mount and dismount your horse while you hold a full bucket of water.

You'll need a long rope on your course for schooling on obstacles that need to be dragged. You may want to school your horse on dragging the sack of cans.

Be sure to scrounge all the big poles you can find for use in all types of obstacles. Quite often, the telephone and power companies replace poles. If you see them doing just that, stop and ask what they plan on doing with the old pole. You'll probably get to take it. A chain saw and a little time can "whittle it down" to trail course size.

A mailbox mounted on a post is good to have on your practice course. Keep something in it, such as a wadded-up tarp, old slicker, or even a newspaper. Vary it often.

The best type of gate to use when first schooling is a large gate. If your horse is ready for a small one, you can usually have a pipe gate made, or you can make another type of portable gate out of wood. The average gate height in the show ring is *supposed* to be about 42 or 43 inches. If you make a portable gate, try to build it with a base set up so that the horse has to walk over the pole at the bottom. This is the type of gate you'll most often run into in the show ring.

Old, abandoned "fake" Christmas trees make excellent variations to obstacles by adding them as "brush." Real branch cuttings from bushes, pine trees, or hedges also work. You'll often run into such things at a show, and your horse should be schooled on them.

It never hurts to have a "wild" animal. Though trail course designers sometimes get carried away and include animals that NO sane person would want his horse to get near, you will, ordinarily, be asked to ride your horse near a barnyard animal. Whenever the possibility arises, get your horse used to being near such animals as goats, chickens, pigs, and cattle. One of the obstacles at the first $2,000 trail horse Grand Prix at the Cow Palace was a pen where the horses were ridden through a gate into the "middle" of several calves. They had to move the calves around the pen and then were ridden out another gate. If this wasn't enough to unnerve a horse that wasn't used to working around cattle, the final obstacle was to ride and stand the horse in a bucking chute with the gate closed, with TWO huge bulls from the bucking string in the adjoining chutes. Trail classes can get a little hectic! Be ready for anything!

Chapter Five

Working Gates

A trail horse should never be taken up to work a gate until he is completely schooled on the body-control movements. He should completely understand the concept of sidepassing, backing easily and turning on the forehand and haunches. This should have been taught *away* from the obstacles.

If a horse hasn't learned the basics before he's started on gates, he's going to want to head straight into the gate, rather than getting parallel to it. He'll swing his rear end out away from it. The more you try to leg him over, the more upset he'll get. Be *sure* to give your horse a chance. He must know the basics. THEN start to work on gates.

5.1. *This is the proper type of gate to use when introducing a green horse to this type of obstacle.*

5.2. *Barbara is circling Dusty.*

The best type of gate to start a young horse on is a wide, sturdy one, such as the big arena gate shown on page 68. This allows a green horse plenty of space to move around in, and he'll be more relaxed about the situation. Dusty, the palomino horse pictured in this chapter, is being schooled on a smaller gate because he has advanced from the beginning stage. Pay close attention to the methods Barbara is using with this horse, because they are not the SAME methods you should use on the *larger* gate when you start your trail horse. When your horse progresses, as Dusty has, then do the same routine that Barbara is doing on a smaller gate.

Do not, at first, attempt to open the gate. Just take the green horse in a big circle near the gate so he can be ridden up and allowed to stand facing it. Nothing else should be done. The horse should be asked to stand there for several minutes and just RELAX. During the next session, repeat this, then make another circle, this time riding up parallel to the gate right into a position which puts your leg at the latch. This rather than sidepassing should be done in the beginning. No sidepassing or pivoting to get closer to the gate to open it should even be attempted if you can just ride up correctly.

During the schooling of a green horse, the first few sessions should be done with the horse being ridden through as the gate is pushed away. Later, you'll learn about how to vary the schooling to keep from training a "one-way" horse, but for now, the push-away-type of working the gate is the easiest for a green horse to understand.

When you've ridden the horse up and he's standing parallel to the gate, just stand there for a few minutes, letting him relax. Don't touch the gate at first. If you use this type of slow schooling with several pauses throughout a horse's career, he'll never try to hurry through obstacles. Stand him there a few minutes, then reach down, rattle the gate a little with your hand, wiggle the latch, and stand some more. The horse shouldn't become so "automatic" that he thinks every time the gate makes a sound, it's time to turn and go through.

When the horse has been standing quietly, reach down and SHOVE THE GATE OPEN. DON'T HOLD ONTO IT—LET IT GO. It's too hard to work a green horse on a gate and do it show ring perfect. Neither one of you need to worry about that now! Push the gate open and stand the horse in his former stance without riding him through until he's been asked to stand quietly for several moments. If you're worried about the gate swinging back, if it's the type which will not remain open on its own, have someone stand on the side opposite the horse and hold the gate.

When you're ready to go through, you must tuck the horse's head. Bring it back to you and back him a couple of steps so he clears the post. Then rein him around and position him PARALLEL to the open gate. This is extremely important. With the exception of the time spent pivoting around the end of the gate, the horse should always remain parallel to it. The hindquarters or front end shouldn't be swung out away from it. You have to school your horse to respond to you so he can be kept parallel at all times.

Ride through a step or two and stop the horse. Let him stand. Next, move him up until your leg clears the end of the gate and stand him again. Remember that you NEVER pivot around the end of the gate until your leg clears.

5.3. He is brought around into a position parallel to the gate. He is NOT sidepassed up when this green.

5.4. Dusty is asked to stand quietly at the gate.

5.5. Barbara will be working a left-handed-push-away, walking through the gate. With a green horse, you start by making him stand while you rattle the gate. This may be the extent of the schooling for the first day. Ride him up and make him stand without actually working the gate.

5.6. When the horse is ready to be ridden through, push the gate away and LET GO! Don't try to hold on to it.

5.7. Tuck the horse's head and stand him in a position parallel to the gate.

5.8. Walk him through a few steps and stop. Then walk him to the point where your leg clears the gate. Barbara's left leg is clear, so she is beginning to bend Dusty around to start the pivot.

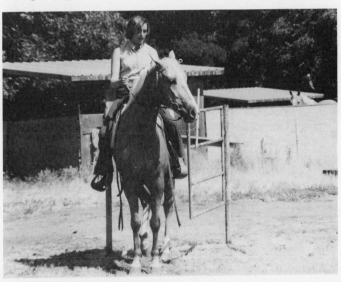

5.9. Part way through the pivot, the horse is stopped to stand.

5.10. He is then taken parallel to the gate, the gate is pushed away (not held on to), and the horse is sidepassed over to it. Notice the up-and-down motion of the rider's right leg to move the horse over.

Your pivot around a gate which has been pushed away from you is, in actuality, a 360-degree turn on the forehand. The horse's front end stays in basically the same position. He is parallel to the gate, say on the right side of it. He then pivots completely around until he is parallel on the left side of the gate. It's a complete rotation around the end of the gate.

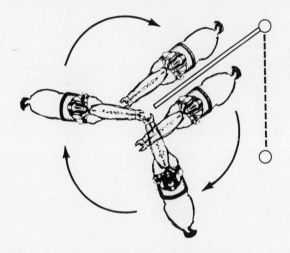

5.A. A right-handed ridethrough, pushing gate away.

With a green horse, you can't expect it to be perfect, but you do the best you can without asking too much of him at first. If he's been taught to turn on the forehand, as he should have been, you just take a light hold on his head to keep him from "leaving the country," and you leg his hindquarters around. He'll have to move his front feet just a little, but he shouldn't make any big moves with them which will put him too far away from the gate.

When you're around to the other side of the gate, push it shut. You don't have to hang on to it. Then, just use your hands and legs to sidepass him over. Keep him parallel to the gate.

5.11. *The rider comes up at an angle.*

5.12. *Here the horse is pivoted parallel to the gate, six or eight inches away. The latch is in easy reach for the rider.*

5.13. *The horse's head is tucked. Notice how the mare remains steady on her back legs and her front end pivots around.*

5.14. *Barbara takes the mare through, keeping her parallel to the gate. Notice the contact with the horse's mouth.*

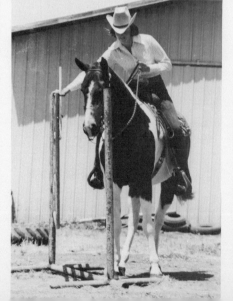 

5.15. The mare is kept parallel, being ridden to the point where the rider's right leg clears the end of the gate. Look at how cleverly the mare is stepping over the base pole with her back foot.

5.16. The front end is steadied and the mare begins to pivot, swinging her hindquarters all the way around to position herself parallel on the opposite side of the gate.

5.17. She is sidepassed over to close the gate and puts the rider in a perfect position at the latch and a good distance from the gate. She's not crowding and, in comparison, isn't so far away from the gate that the rider has to bend over to reach the latch.

After at least several days of this schooling, you should be able to start holding on to the gate a little, increasing your ability gradually until you can hold onto it throughout the opening and closing. A green horse is going to figure out quickly that where the gate goes, he'll also have to go. He saw that when you swung the gate open or swung it closed and made him follow it. Now, as you hold on, he'll have a better understanding of what it's all about.

When the horse is adept at working the push-away gate, you can introduce him to the other ways of working a gate. If you want to teach him to back through, for instance, start with the push-away backthrough. Position him parallel to the gate, swing it open without hanging on, then back him through, take him around, and sidepass him to close it. By using the "start-stop" method of going through the gate, you should produce a horse who is quiet, willing, and confident about gates. Later in this chapter, you will study four of the eight ways to work a gate as shown on a finished horse. You should completely understand each step before trying to work your green horse on any one of them.

The variation of ways to work the gate is very important to the green horse after he has been introduced to the "walk-through-push-away" method. Many people ruin their trail horses by constantly schooling them to work a gate only one way. If a horse works a gate the same way all the time, he does it out of habit rather than by your cues. When he's someday asked to work the gate a new way, he'll blow up because he doesn't understand it. SCHOOL YOUR HORSE ON WORKING THE GATE ALL EIGHT WAYS AND DO IT ON AS MANY DIFFERENT GATES AS POSSIBLE, and in as many different SITUATIONS as possible. Try to use gates at other stables or anyplace where there is a workable gate.

School your horse so that he will be able to handle the portable gates found at most shows. The portable gate (see the photos pp. 76–77) has a base. There is a pole lying across the ground parallel to the bottom pole of the gate. This support pole often confuses a horse not accustomed to it, and you'll see a horse bang it with his feet in the show ring. To teach your horse to feel for it with his feet, or to back over it when working the backthrough gate, make a simulated base on one or two gates you generally school on. Lay a 2×4 or 2×6 on the ground, securing it somehow so it can't be kicked out of the way. It has to be solid enough that a horse learns he can't just push it away easily.

Once your horse is working pretty well on gates, he might get a little sluggish, particularly if he's a lazy type that's a little insensitive. When asking this type of horse to sidepass over to the gate, run your heel and calf up and down or back and forth on his leg, rather than using a straight, steady leg pressure. This arouses the horse and causes him to move. A numb horse will stand all day while you just squeeze his side, but moving your leg will wake him up.

How about Rider Mistakes?

Many riders are in a hurry to work the gate. Even in the show ring, however, you can take your time working the gate without being penalized. So if you must stop for a moment to get your bearings, then do it.

When working a gate, sit square on your horse. Leaning off to the side causes problems. If you're asked to work a low gate and you must reach down, bend your upper body but don't shift the weight in your saddle. Let's look at some of the problems caused when a rider leans over in the saddle, shifting his legs and hips.

The first is connected with riding through the gate, getting ready to push it open away from you. Let's say you're working it right-handed, pushing the gate away with your right hand. The gate is low, so you lean way off to the side of your horse.

Your left leg moves way up, out away from the horse. It should be into his side, holding him near the gate. As the leg moves away, so does the horse. He's free to just walk off to the left while you're pushing the gate to the right. This sends you "South" while your horse goes "North." It's quite possible in this situation for a gate to be tipped over, or for a rider to land on the ground if he's too afraid to let go of the gate.

This problem isn't limited to low gates; it can happen with any size gate, particularly if you don't sidepass your horse in closely. If you have to lean way over to open the gate, your horse can walk off.

5.18. The mare is in a good position, and the rider can reach the latch while sitting square in the saddle.

5.19. *As the gate is swung over, the mare is sidepassed. She's now being moved up a little, getting somewhat out of the parallel position so she can start her pivot.*

5.20. *When the rider's leg clears, the mare's front end is held still and the back end pivots all the way around until it is parallel to the opposite side of the gate.*

5.21. *The rider continues to open the gate so it is wide enough to pass through. The mare has about one more step to the left with her hindquarters and she will be perfectly parallel.*

5.22. *Maintaining mouth contact, Barbara rides the mare through, sliding her right hand up on the gate.*

5.22A. *Without taking her hand off the gate, she sidepasses the mare over to close and latch the gate.*

Leaning can also cause the reverse of the above. Let's say you are working the gate the same way—right-handed, pushing it away from you. As you lean too far over, your *right* leg goes into the horse. Your left leg has been telling him to sidepass up to the gate, and now your right leg is telling him "no . . . move back over." This contradiction can make a horse blow up.

Horse and rider "separation" also occurs when the rider asks the horse to pivot around the end of the gate and doesn't have his leg in tight against the horse. Excess leaning takes the leg away and the horse can walk right off.

A rider should also be careful never to push down on portable gates while working them, for they can easily tip. Older gates also tend to want to fall down on the hinges and swing away from you. What's the remedy? Open the gate and keep your hand on it, holding it up if necessary. Remember that on a finished horse and in the show ring, you should never turn loose of the gate. You work the latch, slide your hand down the gate as it opens, hold the end as you pivot around, then slide your hand back up as you close the gate and work the latch. Never turn loose of the gate until the latch is secured.

When you work a gate, keep your reins short. You don't need to pull on your horse, but keep the reins short enough that you can restrict his head, gather him up, or back with very little movement of the hand. Many riders just throw the horse's head away while working a gate, and there's no control during the pivot or sidepassing.

Crowding the gate is a common problem seen in show ring trail classes. Some judges will knock down for it, some won't, but to be safe, you shouldn't let your horse crowd the gate. What's it caused by? If you leg your horse too hard and don't let up soon enough, you're going to sidepass him into the gate too closely. If he wants to go in on his own and crowd, you have to push him with your inside leg to hold him from moving in too close. Remember that a judge wants to see a horse approach the gate smoothly, not fighting his rider. The horse should accept the whole thing. He should put his rider right up to the latch so it's an easy reach. This approach can be done by coming in at an angle or sidepassing right in, but when you get parallel to the gate, you should stop when your horse is a distance of six or eight inches from it. The smooth way to do this would be to ride up on an angle, heading in and stopping when your leg is right at the latch. Then all you'd need to do is to pivot his hindquarters over so he becomes parallel. If you overturn, he crowds the gate. If you ride up out of position, then have to stop, ride up, ride back, or move him out away from the gate and bring him back in, it distracts from the smoothness you're trying to convey.

Remember—you have to worry about crowding both when you come in to open the gate and when you sidepass over to close it. It will take a lot of work on your part and a lot of schooling for your horse to smooth out your gate work. It's a big part of every trail course, so it's important to do it right. If you have a horse that someone else broke to work gates, you may have an extra problem to work on.

Cowboy-broke ranch horses that have been worked with cattle are notorious gate-crowders. They've always been taken right up to a gate and asked to squeeze right into it to help hold cattle in the chutes or pens. You have to reschool a horse like this by treating him as a green horse. Take him up to the gate without actually working it, use your hands and legs to position him, and spend a lot of time just holding him there. Then, proceed as with the regular green-horse schooling.

5.23. The horse has been ridden up into good position, and the rider's leg is right at the latch. The horse is just a few inches away from the gate, perfectly parallel. Reins are held in the right hand for this method, because it is left-handed gate-work.

5.24. The horse was ridden up until her rear end cleared the post. *This is important! She is then put into a parallel-to-the-gate side-pass and begins backing. Rider keeps the gate open WIDE.*

5.25. *When the rider's left leg clears the end of the gate, the horse begins a pivot. Her front end remains still and her hindquarters rotate around to the other side. Notice the rider's contact with the horse's mouth.*

5.26. When parallel to the gate, the sidepass over to close is started.

5.27. The mare is just a few inches away and is not crowding the gate while Barbara works the latch.

Be Ready for Gate Variations in the Show Ring

Gates are often dressed up with spooky things such as plastic tarps and hides, sometimes *fresh* hides, hung over the gate. Sometimes, you'll be asked to work a jump and stop which is just before the gate and puts you right in, head on to the gate center. In this case, you hold your horse a few moments to settle him, then pivot him around into position to work the gate.

Some judges ask that you jog to the gate. How you do this depends a lot on your horse. If he's real well broke, it looks flashy if you just jog right up and stop in perfect position, with your leg at the latch and your horse six or eight inches away from the gate perfectly parallel. With a horse that's somewhat green, it's best to jog up just until you feel him getting a little

5.28. *The rider has opened the gate and sidepassed the mare over and is now backing her up to prepare for a pivot which would put the mare's hindquarters in a position to pass backwards through the gate. When working gates,* THE GATE MUST BE OPENED WIDE ENOUGH TO GIVE THE HORSE PLENTY OF ROOM.

5.29. *The mare has overshot a little, so will have to be stepped up one step, sidepassed over to the left a little to clear the pole, then she can back through.*

5.30. *Now in proper position parallel to the gate, the mare can easily back through. Notice the way the rider holds the romel and reins in the right hand to keep them from dropping down.*

5.31. *As the mare backs, Barbara keeps her left hand on the gate, sliding it back.*

5.32. *The mare is kept parallel and the gate is pulled to close it. Barbara slides her hand up to the latch to secure the gate.*

apprehensive. Break to a walk a few steps before the gate and take him in that way. With either horse, after he is standing in position to begin working the gate, hold him there long enough to settle him before reaching for the latch.

Many shows set up an obstacle which you are IN as soon as you close the gate. It's almost always a straight backthrough or an L that starts parallel to the gate. Horses often don't realize they're in another obstacle. They're used to being brought up to something, maneuvered into the entrance, and asked to work it separately from other obstacles. You could school the horse at home for this situation by holding him still after closing the gate (which you should always do anyway!), then slowly and carefully backing him straight away from the gate. Include this occasionally in your schooling so your horse won't get in the habit of leaving the gate the same way every time.

Some of the bigger California shows have recently come up with a real mind boggler which confuses even the best horses! The gate is *open* on the course, and riders are asked to jog or long trot their horses *right through* the open gate! Often, there is a series of cavelletti, trot-over poles, placed before and after the gate. Most of the horses presented with this trot-through-gate refuse it because they've been brainwashed to stop at every gate and work it. It would be clever on your part if, at home, you occasionally rode your horse through an open gate so he'd understand it in case you're ever asked to do it at a show.

Remember that there are EIGHT WAYS TO WORK A GATE. Five of these are shown in the photos in this chapter. The remaining three can be made by working each one of these from the opposite side. In other words, you can work a gate any one of these ways, depending on the instructions you get from the judge. Because you'll never be sure what you'll be asked for, you must be versed in all eight ways. If the judge does NOT stipulate the way, leaving it up to you, the proper way would be to ride through and push the gate away from you. Here are the eight ways to work a gate:

1. Right-handed ridethrough, pushing gate away. (See photos of Pinto mare, p. 76.)

2. Left-handed ridethrough, pushing gate away. (See photos of Palomino horse, p. 71.)

3. Right-handed ridethrough, pulling gate toward you. (See photos of Pinto mare, p. 80.)

4. Left-handed ridethrough, pulling gate toward you.

5. Right-handed backthrough, pushing gate away.

6. Left-handed backthrough, pushing gate away. (See photos of Pinto mare, p. 85.)

7. Right-handed backthrough, pulling gate toward you.

8. Left-handed backthrough, pulling gate toward you. (See photos of Pinto mare, p. 88.)

Chapter Six

Stepovers

Call them stepovers, or walkovers, the fact remains that a horse who drops his head down to investigate this type of obstacle and works it neatly is going to score beautifully! You can school a trail horse to work these obstacles in such an impressive manner that he'll give the appearance of searching out spacing and investigating each part of the stepover because of natural caution—even if there's not an ounce of it in his soul!

The methods for starting a trail horse on stepovers are controversial. Some trainers swear by riding them over first. Others feel confidence comes from leading them over. Still others start a horse, particularly a young horse, by ground-driving them. Because all the systems are varied, it's important to explain each method to you. Each horse is an individual. It's up to you to "feel out" your horse's attitude and ability and pick the method you think will work best on him. Before we take a look at the three basic ways to start a horse on stepovers, it's important to explain the systems of cuing from the saddle, so the variance in photos in this chapter doesn't confuse you.

You'll see riders using different styles of riding to cue their horses for stepovers. Some come way up and out of the saddle, over the horse's neck. Some sit up fairly straight and only release the head. Some bend forward just slightly while dropping the reins down on the neck. It seems as though each individual rider comes up with his individual "style." Some training stables teach all their students to cue the same way, and you can easily spot a student from a particular stable by his method of riding in approaching a stepover.

The important thing in cuing a horse is not so much HOW you do it, but how you do it in contrast to other cues. You have to be *consistent* in your cue. The cue for stepovers must be different from the cue for a jump. If a horse doesn't know the difference in your cues, he's likely to jump a stepover, or step over a jump! Quite often, in a show holding more than one trail class, an obstacle will be changed. What is a jump in the first class might be a stepover in the next. If you cue your horse the same way in each class, he's going to do the obstacle the same way, even though it's supposed to be different.

Your cue shouldn't interfere with your horse's ability to balance and work the obstacle. Many young riders today are seen going over the horse's neck, leaning way off to the SIDE. This can cause a horse to swerve off to the side of his obstacle, making it difficult for him to work. Also take into consideration what works best for your horse. If your horse is heavy in front and inclined to be somewhat clumsy with his front feet, you wouldn't want to lean way over his neck. A horse carries two-thirds of his weight on his front feet. If a clumsy horse has your weight added to that, he's not going to be too lightfooted in front! If he's not clumsy, he should be able to handle a lean-over cue.

Remember these two basics on cuing a horse. For a stepover, lean forward—just a little or way over—and give the horse his head. He's sensitive. He can feel your weight shift as you come over his neck. For a jump, a horse should be gathered up a little, with light contact on his mouth at the approach, the rider sitting erect in the saddle, clucking to the horse as an additional cue. As the horse gets up to the jump, the rider can release the reins enough to allow the horse to use his head and neck for balance, and to avoid jerking on the horse's mouth during the jump. When the horse leaves the ground, the thrust is going to send you forward, as it does to an English rider on a hunter or jumper. This is acceptable. Just be sure you don't lean forward prematurely, or your horse might get his cues mixed up.

When do you cue? Whether you're working with a green horse, or are performing in the show ring on a finished one, you have to know when to cue. You should let the horse know what's coming anywhere from six to ten feet ahead of an obstacle. Though you may use some "stop-start" schooling at home, though you plan on stopping him in front of the obstacle to slow him down and make him work it more carefully, he still has to know it's a stepover. In the show ring, however, you must just cue him and keep going. Judges today are often calling a stepover a refusal if the horse is ridden up and the rider *stops,* drops the horse's head, then goes over. When you're showing, keep the forward motion.

When do you stop your cue? Never stop until your horse has cleared the obstacle with both his front AND back feet. If you're working a six-pole stepover, for instance, and the horse's front feet have cleared the pole, and you go back to a normal body position, the cue is gone, so the horse will raise his head. When his head goes up, his back feet go *down,* and he'll hit the obstacle with them. This rule applies to both schooling and showing! Now that you understand the importance of a definite cue, and how to use it, lets look at the methods of starting a horse on stepovers.

GROUND-DRIVING OVER STEPOVERS

This method is particularly helpful if you have an unstarted colt who is old enough to saddle and drive. If you work him over simple stepovers in this way, by the time he's ready to ride, he'll have all his basics down.

6.1. With some horses, ground-driving is a good way to start working simple logs. Three Chants is going over a natural log.

Driving over obstacles is also an advantage with a horse who is a little balky and who doesn't want to cooperate while being led over. Have you ever seen a person teach a horse to lead in the trailer by driving the horse with lines? This is the same idea. When you're behind a horse and can slap the lines gently at his sides, there is quite a bit of reasoning for him to move forward! It's often a lot easier to "push" a balky horse than to "pull" him. If he tries to duck out the side of an obstacle, you can back him up to get him straight and send him at it again. Using wings on the side of a long pole will discourage him from ducking out, and your hands, when properly used on the lines, will encourage him to move forward.

When driving over obstacles, you would follow the same basic progression of starting with one log and gradually increasing, as used in the riding-over method.

Leading over Stepovers

Many trainers feel leading a horse over obstacles is the best method going for instilling confidence. A horse has a special kind of security when you're down there by his head. Leading-over is also a good way to slow down a horse that wants to rush, because if YOU slow down, so will he.

When you start leading over obstacles, you should begin with a long obstacle that will encourage the horse to go over, rather than around. You need enough room that BOTH of you can step over it. The theory with leading-over is that YOU do what you want the horse to do! You have to go over with him. If you went off to the side, he'd want to do the same thing. He follows you. Remember that since you're trying to get him to drop his head and look at the obstacle, you must do the same. As you approach the obstacle, lean way over and slowly walk up and carefully step over the log or pole. It looks ridiculous, but it works! In the photos on page 98, I am working the chestnut gelding, Three Chants, over simple logs. He is extremely green, but still gets the idea and drops his head a little as I bend down and cross the logs with him. During his schooling, I used the word "down" when I bent over, asking him to drop his head. Even when walking out in the open, away from obstacles, I can bend down while walking, tell him "down," and he'll lower his head and keep it there as long as I'm down. The horse can even get the idea of dropping his head from your voice, so the transition from leading over to riding over won't be as confusing.

You'll notice in the photos on p. 98 that even after Chant had stepped over the log with his front feet, I remained down and asked him to keep his head down. This is to avoid having him raise his head and "lower" his back feet, hitting the log with them as he attempted to stepover.

When you're working a horse on leadover work, you would begin with a simple single log and progress much the same as with the rideover schooling.

Riding over Stepovers from the Beginning

In the beginning, the important thing is to keep the forward motion, to be sure a horse won't refuse on a simple stepover. Start schooling on something fairly substantial, such as a tele-

6.2. Bending down and stepping over the obstacle yourself encourages the horse to do the same. Chant is bringing his head down fairly well in this basic work.

6.3. Keep down! If you stand up before the horse's back legs are over the obstacle, he'll raise his head, causing his back legs to hit the log.

phone pole or large log. It has to be something the horse can't knock down or easily roll out of the way. He'll learn from the start that if he doesn't pick his feet up, he'll bump them against the log. This beginning obstacle should also be wide enough that the horse doesn't think he can duck off to the side. If you don't have an extremely long log or pole, add wings to the side—heavy poles set up on the ends of the obstacles, running parallel to the horse's position. If you can just get a horse to go over an obstacle a few times to give him the idea of what he's supposed to do, he'll stop trying to duck out, and you'll be able to remove the wings. He won't be scared of the obstacle because he'll know what it's there for.

You should get in the habit of using your legs a great deal in encouraging a horse to head for the center of the obstacle and work it straight. If he starts to duck off a little to the left, apply pressure with your left leg. If he's hesitant about going over the obstacle, apply pressure with both legs to drive him forward.

A horse has to be completely sure of himself in working a single stepover before you try anything more difficult. You then work up *extremely gradually*. Introduce a second pole or log by placing it two strides away from the first. This gives a horse a chance to have enough room in between to concentrate on one at a time. He maneuvers the first one, gathers himself up, then goes over the second. Because of the spacing, it's not difficult for him, and he gains confidence in himself and in you. Later, you can ask him to work those two stepovers with tighter spacing, placing them just one stride apart. IF the horse seems very sure of himself, you can add one log at a time until he is working a series of four or five poles, evenly spaced at one or two strides apart—whatever you feel the horse is capable of.

How do you figure the striding? The easiest way is to lay one log or pole down and watch while someone leads your

6.4. *A stout log or telephone pole is a good starter obstacle, when riding a green trail horse over stepovers. Lew Silva takes Flaxie over a single log.*

horse over it and goes in a straight line away from it. You can easily see where the horse is *naturally* stepping, because you don't want him to have to shorten a stride or take an extra-long step to work a pole. Look for where his feet fall and place your poles so he just "walks right along" without having any trouble getting over them. He's not yet ready for the tougher spacing. Things first have to be very simple for him if he's to gain, and keep, his confidence. Some horses have terrific coordination and take to stepovers naturally, progressing at a rapid rate. Most, however, need an extremely slow progression. Never push your green trail horse beyond his capabilities!

WHEN HE'S READY FOR AN INCREASE IN DIFFICULTY

A horse has to learn to handle his own feet. You can't move them for him. You teach him to become clever by schooling him on enough different things that he learns he's going to hit them with his feet if he doesn't work them carefully. A horse with sensitive legs makes a top stepover horse, because he doesn't want anything touching him. You'll find that a lot of trainers are convinced stocking-legged horses are more sensitive because of the lighter pigmented skin on their legs. This isn't always the case, but is a great deal of the time. A lot of dark-legged horses are also sensitive.

Lighter poles, such as jump poles, can be substituted fairly soon for the telephone poles and logs if your horse is sensitive and has the ability to work something smaller. Anything smaller than a jump pole should be postponed until later.

You can now begin both varying your spacing and using several different types of poles or logs in one stepover combination. You're now starting to make him clever. He has to learn to pick his way through anything. Use pole and tire combinations, or poles that are big and bulky teamed with 4×4 posts and jump poles. Be sure he has been completely

6.5. After a while, a green horse should be able to work a series of poles, set one stride apart, in his natural striding. Make it easy for him at first!

schooled on tires as a single obstacle before asking him to work a stepover-tire combination.

When you're beginning to increase the difficulty, you can elevate alternate ends of the poles, such as shown in the photos in the obstacle that Mock Won is working on page 108. This tight spacing is quite advanced, but you could set up the same type of obstacle with greater spacing for the less finished horse, gradually taking him up to the tight spacing. Start putting a tarp under your poles, or spread a little brush on the ground so the horse must look very carefully to see where to place his feet.

The word "GRADUAL," when increasing difficulty, just can't be overstressed here. Making things too difficult, too soon, can ruin any trail horse. If he starts seeming a little too clumsy, it's a good indication that (a) he just isn't ready for that obstacle, or (b) your spacing is off and he just can't make the reaches, or (c) he can't collect his stride up and shorten it for this type of obstacle. In the last case, reset your obstacle and "back off" a little so you don't lose his confidence. Though he might not be able to work a certain obstacle today, he might catch on and be able to handle it next week, or even tomorrow. It's up to you to pace his progress.

6.6. The Horseradish Kid is being taken over a two-log-one-tire combination with spacing so he has to use a long stride. He wasn't one to drop his head down naturally, as you can see, and was later taught with the use of a bat.

6.7. When a horse requires "artificial" schooling to get a head to drop "naturally," begin by GENTLY tapping the horse on the poll with a crop.

6.8. When the horse gives to the crop and drops his head, even if only a few inches, he should be petted.

6.9. *The transition should eventually allow you to drop the horse's head anytime, anyplace, by just moving your hand forward and down on his neck. But, in a class do NOT touch the neck.*

Whether working stepovers at home or in the show ring, you have to help your horse by judging the spacing to make the proper approach. If the spacing is wide, give the horse plenty of room before going over. This sets a good, bold stride so he can handle the reaches in the long spacing. If the obstacle is a tightly spaced one, you have to gather your horse, collect him up, and be sure he's geared down to enter it slowly and carefully with short steps. You have to adjust the stride long before you come up to the obstacle in order to work it correctly. You can't ask a horse to stretch out in a long-strided approach, then suddenly cramp up into tightly spaced poles. At the same time, you can't creep him up, then ask him to work a boldly spaced stepover that will require him to reach a great deal.

6.10. This type of spacing is a beginning in getting a horse to become clever on his stepovers. It's also a good obstacle to practice, for the spacing is often used in the show ring.

6.11. Walkovers are often made more difficult by the alternate raising of the ends of the poles. Flaxie takes a good look.

WHAT IS DONE WITH THE HORSE THAT RUSHES HIS STEPOVERS?

When you're schooling a green horse, you hope that he won't rush, because you don't want anything except good forward motion. If you have to stop him, you might start his causing to refuse. The fact remains, though, that if he IS rushing, something must be done about it. Often, the more finished horse, who didn't rush when he was green, will start it as a method to get over the obstacle quickly and "get it done." He might not be paying enough attention to what he's doing. This is where the "stop-start" schooling begins.

Ground-work often helps the rushing, green horse. He's

6.12. This is a tightly spaced obstacle for a more finished horse.

6.13. Mock Won has approached the obstacle and has dropped his head. He negotiates it well, but just a bit faster than he should have.

going to do what YOU do, and if you step over the obstacle with him, he'll pace himself at your speed. Try working a green horse on the ground, and if he tries to rush when you lead him up to the obstacle, *very calmly* stop him and back him up about ten feet, holding him there for a few moments. Notice the words "very calmly." If you made a big deal out of this, and jerked the horse's shank and ran him back, he'd become a nervous wreck at the obstacle. By stopping and quietly backing him, you're simply saying that he can't go over until he slows down and does it right, and that you have the patience to quietly move back all day! He WANTS to go forward, and he has to learn that he won't get to go forward until he does it right.

Let's examine "stop-start" schooling from the saddle. If your horse is pretty well schooled, but has the tendency to move too quickly over his stepovers, you have to work carefully at getting him to slow down. In the photos on pages 108 to 111, you see the palomino gelding, Mock Won, going over a series of five poles. He did a good job of working the poles, with the exception that he could have gone just a *little* slower. After being walked over the obstacles to the right, he is reversed and brought back, to go over to your left. A few feet before the obstacle, he is stopped and asked to stand with his head down. He has stopped on the command "WHOA." To take hold of his head at this point would cause him to pick his head way up and lose his concentration. This is where obedience to voice commands is so essential. As you can see, he is standing quietly, looking carefully at what he's going to step over.

Next, he is taken almost to the first pole and stopped again, still being signalled to keep his head down. He's stepped over the first pole, then stopped again and asked to stand for a minute or more. He takes another step forward when the rider gently legs him up, stops one more time, then is allowed to step the rest of the way out. What happens here? The horse

6.14. *He is reversed and brought around to try it again in the "stop-start" method of schooling. He is stopped in front of the obstacle on voice command and made to drop his head and stand.*

6.15. *He is then inched up a little closer and stopped again on voice.*

6.16. *After stepping over the first pole, he is stopped again. His head remains down.*

6.17. *One more step, then another stop.*

6.18. Slowly, he completes the obstacle.

learns to relax, not to rush. He'll slow down and pay attention to EACH pole. The next time you ride him straight through, he'll do it more carefully. He'll know how to slow down and relax, and, quite possibly, he'll be waiting for you to stop him.

VARIANCE KEEPS A HORSE INTERESTED!

Throughout your schooling, you have to be especially careful to vary your obstacles. While a green horse often works on simple rows, a horse, as he advances, starts working a little bit of everything. A horse is more inclined to drop his head and look naturally if he's going over an obstacle that's new to him. That's one reason so many horses look closer at obstacles in the show ring than at home. If you worked the exact same poles with the exact same spacing on all your schooling sessions at home, you'd be creating a horse that worked that obstacle out of habit, and wouldn't be able to work anything else. Vary your obstacles as much as possible. Set up something different each day. Paint your poles different colors and wrap

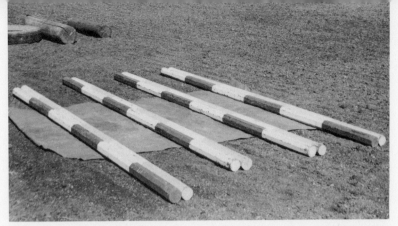

6.19. These four "double poles" are placed on a tarp. Horses must be schooled at home for such variations. Many horses need a lot of work to get them to accept stepping on plastic.

aluminum foil around parts of them. Change the *place* you work your horse as often as possible. Even if it's a few feet away, it breaks the routine.

GETTING THEM TO DROP THEIR HEADS AND "LOOK"

It is a fairy tale to assume that every green horse will approach his first stepover and drop his nose clear down to touch it. It just doesn't happen. You're going to have to work at in-

6.20. Blue Frost B accepts the tarp and works the obstacle perfectly.

stilling in him the idea that he should investigate the obstacles closely. Eventually he'll do it on his own. If you have trouble getting the idea across, you can resort to what is almost considered trick training—getting him to drop his head on a voice command or cue. There are what I call "artificial" ways to get a horse to drop his head and keep it down. Each horse is an individual, and you have to test him to find out what will work best. Many training stables stick with only one method and can't imagine any other. It works for them because their trainer is using it, or is standing right there while the students try it. When you're "on your own," however, it's best to experiment with different ways until you see which one will work on your horse.

"The Bribe System"

I've had two horses that were deluxe eaters— they'd do anything for a carrot! Standing alongside the horse, you squat down so you can hold the carrot on the ground, giving the verbal command "down." When the horse drops his head, he gets the carrot. It's as simple as that. You're trying to get him to drop his head on a verbal command, and he's rewarded with food. After awhile, try it from the saddle by just telling him "down" and if you get a reaction, pet him. No food, just petting. Then, start cuing him for a stepover, such as leaning forward and dropping the reins on his neck as you say "down." Hopefully, he'll start dropping his head on the rein cue.

The Old "Search-for-Food" Method

Scattering grain or carrot pieces in the obstacle will cause a horse to drop his head and search for chow. Since he'll never know exactly when and where he's going to find the food, he'll start looking everything over.

"Sniffing" the Obstacles

When your stepover series is set up, "paint" each log with

something that has a different odor. You can use a little hoof dressing, coat spray, bacon grease, or whatever has a distinctive smell. You need only a small amount on the log or pole top. The horse will begin to smell the stepovers and, hopefully, dropping his head to investigate will become a habit.

Making It a Little Tough

When a horse is working a series of poles and is capable, but is not watching where he's going on four or five stepovers, scrounge around until you can get as many as twenty poles and logs and set them up at varied spacing. Make a long row, some one stride apart, some two. Set up a break of four or five feet in between two. When a horse has this many to walk over, he'll learn after the first few that he'd better keep a close eye on where he's going!

Using a Crop or Bat to Lower the Head

If this method isn't done correctly, you'll produce a mad and headshy horse. Don't bash your horse on the head with the bat! Do as explained here and as shown in the photos.

Take your horse away from the obstacles. Lightly tap and "tickle" the horse between his ears with a bat or crop. At the same time, move your rein hand down on his neck as an alternate cue. The INSTANT the horse ducks his head, even a tiny bit to get away from the bat, stop touching him with it and pet him. This isn't a one-day thing! Schooling has to be gradual. Each time you work on it, ask him for a little more. As you can see by the expression of the horse in the photos (see pp. 104 and 105), he isn't the least bit upset over it—because it's being done properly.

Do a little each day. Tap his head, get a reaction, stop and pet him. That's enough. As he begins to understand what you're after, you ask for more, getting him to lower his head more, holding it down as long as the bat is held over his head.

6.21. *Poles are often teamed up with tires in show ring obstacles. Notice how a horse would have to vary his stride on this one—a short step over the first log, longer reach into the tire, and another short step to place a foot in between the last two poles.*

What you're after is a tie-in between setting your hand up on his neck and the use of the crop. If he feels your rein hand move at first, he'll know the crop is coming, and he should start dropping his head on the rein cue alone. You should *eventually* be able to take him anyplace, anytime, and get him to drop his head by cuing him with your rein hand.

Once he's working well, you can take him up to an obstacle, holding the bat just in case he needs it, and ask him to stand quietly with his head dropped before you let him go over. Use the bat and your rein hand to cue him to keep his head down until he's off the obstacle with both his front and back feet.

LEADING OVER STEPOVERS IN THE SHOW RING

Many shows require obstacles to be worked with the rider on the ground, leading the horse. Someday you may be asked to lead your horse over a complete set of poles, or an even tougher obstacle. One year at the Cow Palace, riders had to ride through half the obstacle, dismount on the "wrong" side, and go around to the left side of the horse to lead him off.

6.22. *Good News does a fine job of working this obstacle.*

Most of the horses went clean, but the RIDERS often tripped, knocking down the poles, and losing any chance of scoring well on the obstacle. Don't get lazy! Step over each obstacle, paying close attention to what you're doing!

TROTOVERS

This is an obstacle very similar to the caveletti schooling given to hunters and jumpers. The poles, for the horse to trot over, are spaced about four feet apart. Since your horse may not be coordinated at first, you begin by teaching him to trot over a single pole, gradually building up to as many as six or more.

Cues are very important in trotovers, especially if this obstacle is teamed up with something such as a jump. As you can see in the photos on page 119, one show had a series of four trotover poles followed by a jump two strides away, and an immediate stop after the jump. If your cue for stepovers is leaning forward out of the saddle a little, or going way up on the neck, you would have to use it while trotting over the poles. This would leave VERY little time before the jump to change the cue, such as sitting up and lifting the horse's head

6.23. *This rider has chosen to collect her horse up for the trotovers in preparation for the oncoming jump.*

6.24. *The mare completes the trotovers and jumps and stops calmly before the ground pole.*

6.25. *Opie's Misty is moved out a little faster by rider Kathy Cromwell in comparison to the roan horse. Kathy changes her cue with perfect timing.*

6.26. *The mare makes her jump.*

for the jump. The biggest mistake in this show was made in riders not changing their cue or not changing it fast enough. If no change was done, the horse would just keep trotting and stride over the jump, rather than actually jumping it. If a cue WAS done, but the rider waited until it was too late, the horse didn't make an honest jump. He just went over with his front feet, not picking up his back ones until the front hit the ground on the other side.

When you school at home for trotovers and stepovers, you have to be ready for anything!

6.27. *Be ready for anything! This stepover was made complicated by the way the alternate poles were elevated, and the task of leading another horse over the obstacle.*

6.28. Wendy Daniels and Candy Bar work a fairly simple stepover at the Fresno Horse Trials.

6.29. At the Junior Grand National at the Cow Palace, Wendy and Candy were the only ones to make it "clean" through this tough obstacle of highly elevated poles.

Chapter Seven

Tires

Tires and their combination with other types of obstacles make up the more imaginative obstacles you can ask a horse to work. Sometimes a trail course will have a straight row which your horse is to walk, hitting each tire dead center with a foot. Pivots in tractor tires are commonly asked for, sometimes with the front feet in the tire, often with the back feet in. Tires are often mixed with stepovers or placed on bridges or in water boxes. Whatever the type of tire obstacle, there's no way your horse will be ready for it unless he is schooled slowly, learning to accept the one-tire concept before he's asked to do anything else.

Some horses are quite afraid to place a foot in a tire for fear of hanging up a pastern on the rim. If a horse's foot isn't in just right and he tries to pull it back out, he'll hook up and drag the tire toward him. This can cause a minor disaster with a fairly spooky horse, and he'll be afraid to go near the tire again. This happened to one of our horses before we bought him, and it took three months of patience to get him to relax, accept the tire, and place his feet in the center. Since he was so afraid, we spent a lot of time putting feed on the tire and in its center, just letting him eat at the tire and relax. To avoid going through this vigil, if you have such a naturally nervous horse (one like ours with a disgustingly good memory) take special care not to let him get hung up on a tire during the schooling.

The first concept a horse must learn is to walk up to any tire anyplace and put his front feet in it. The easiest way to do this is to scatter tires randomly around your practice course so all he sees and has to concentrate on is one tire at a time. Use large-centered tires at first that are not as high as big tractor tires. Height would discourage a horse from the beginning.

Lead your horse up to the tire and let him take a look at it. Gentle, quiet horses usually pay it little attention. More spooky horses might give you that "who-are-you-kidding" look and do anything possible to avoid touching the tire or putting a foot in it. Try standing your horse there long enough to relax him, then take one foot and try placing it *dead center* in the tire. If he puts his weight down and accepts it, pet him and let him stand there quietly before walking around to place the other foot in. If you try moving him around more quickly, he's likely to dart back. Give him time to relax and accept the idea before placing the other foot in. If, at any time, he should move a foot back and place it on the rim, immediately put the foot in its former position. Always make him stand for a while with both feet in the tire so he gets the idea that he's not to rush out of it.

If you repeat this process several times, you should soon be able to lead the horse up to the tire and ask him to place his feet in on his own. When he's this far along, *then* you start mild discipline if he gets lazy and steps on the rim. Back him up *quietly*, at least for several feet, then bring him back up. Each time he steps on the rim, back him up. It won't take him long to learn that if he doesn't do it right, he won't go forward and get it over with.

Don't rush any progression of schooling on tires. Be sure

7.1. The first thing a horse must learn is to place his feet in any single tire at any location. You start by manually placing his feet in a tire.

you can lead your horse up to a tire anywhere and have him walk right in it. He must learn on several different tires in different locations to teach him that *all* tires must be stepped in, not just one at a certain place. One of the leading trail horse trainers in California says she can even draw a circle with a stick in the dirt and her horses will walk up and step in the circle's center. *That's* when you know they have the concept!

7.2. As he progresses, you should be able to ride him up to any tire, anyplace, and have him step in it. This horse is "feeling" for the tire center with his right front foot.

7.3. *If your weight is not evenly distributed right in the center of the saddle, or if your upper body is shifted, it can throw your horse off balance.*

Use large-centered tires. Set up two tires about one and one-half to two feet apart. Ride or lead the horse up to the first one, get his feet in the center, then stop. Wait a few moments, then ride or lead him to the second. This is the introduction to a tire series and a chance for him to learn some coordination before a more difficult series is put before him. Your switch from leading to riding over the tire obstacles will depend solely on when you think your horse is ready. If he was at the point where you could ride him to any single tire and have him place his feet in it, then he should be ready for introduction to a tire series while you're in the saddle.

Go from two *spread* tires to three, spacing them evenly with enough distance between them for him to walk without worrying about placing his foot in a hole. That gives him a little more time to get coordinated and to think.

Keep in mind that this schooling should be spread out over

7.4. A "spaced series" is an introduction to walking a row of tires. Start with two well-spaced tires and build to three or more.

7.5. DON'T ride your horse up to a row, stop him, then ask him to walk the tires.

7.6. DO walk him up so he can set a pace. Give him his head at least six to ten feet before the tires so he is free to look for the center of the first one.

7.7. *Keep his head loose as he walks the row.*

7.8. *This horse is cheating! Since he wants to step off to the left of the last tire, he is being reined and legged back to the right.*

weeks, even months if necessary. If you rush a horse into tire work, he can quickly sour on it and become clumsy out of resentment. Be VERY sure he's ready to accept walking a series before you ever try riding him over it. Start with two tires placed together and spend days or weeks building up to a row of four or five.

Your approach to the tires will have a lot to do with whether or not your horse can successfully maneuver them. While in the early schooling you walked him up to a single tire and let him look before placing his feet to walk a row, you must now bring him up at a steady pace. He has to *rate and pace himself* into this type of obstacle, and your job is to sit still in the saddle, give him his head at least six to ten feet before the first tire, and not interfere with him as he walks the row. The exception here would be the problem with the horse in the photos on page 129 who likes to make a mild attempt to duck off to the side. In this case, you leg the horse to keep him straight so he has to start that row of tires dead center and not from an angle.

Mixing tires with stepovers is an excellent way to make a horse think about what he's doing. The photo on page 131 shows the tire and one log part of an obstacle. For this particular obstacle, he must concentrate first on the post set on a tarp, then look at the next log, then search for the dead center of the tire, then walk off over the next log. These are fairly advanced problems for a horse to work out AFTER he's had all the basics on both tires and stepovers.

Placing a tire on a bridge is a common obstacle, and it's very impressive when a horse steps right up on the bridge and negotiates it and the tire well. Leading him over the bridge first, asking him to step into the tire, will be a big help. If he steps on the tire rim, stop him. Back him just enough to get his foot behind the tire so he can "start all over and

7.9. *Mixing tires with stepovers varies the schooling and helps a horse become clever and coordinated.*

do it right." Placing a tire right before or after a bridge is another common obstacle. Some horses are a little shaky about accepting a new bridge, much less one with a tire by it, so you need to teach your horse to slow down, relax, and accept the obstacle. Lead him up to the tire, if it's before the step-up, and place his feet in it. Let him stand there quietly. Lead him up onto the bridge and stand him there several minutes so he doesn't get the idea he can jump off. If the tire is at the "step-down" side, gather him up so you can get his front feet in the tire and STOP him while his back feet are still on the bridge. This teaches him that he can't "jump" off the bridge without trouble. He has to learn to take it easy, go quietly, and NOT skip the tire. You should only have to do this three

7.10. *Placing a tire on a bridge is a good practice obstacle, for it is often found in shows.*

or four times before trying, without stops, to negotiate it all in one trip. If he gets hyper, go back to the "start-stop" method and use it until he accepts the idea to go slow and not skip the tire. You want him READY for that show when this obstacle comes up!

Use tires at home in every conceivable obstacle combination you can think of, and vary them so the horse doesn't get bored. Occasionally place a piece of plastic tarp or aluminum foil in a tire center. Put something "crinkly" in the tire center so it makes a noise when he steps in it. He'll be waiting for that at the next one and will maneuver it more carefully. Put a tire in a water box, mix tires with stepovers, and if you're brave, place a tire on a hide!

When your horse is doing a terrific job on the tires, introduce him to the double, or stacked tire. Place a car tire on

7.11. When the horse is working single tires well, introduce him to double or stacked tires. Some shows call for the trail horses to walk a full row of double tires.

7.12. Start teaching the pivot in a tire by leading the horse up and placing his front feet in the center.

top of another of equal size and start him with one double tire at a time until he can work it well, gradually building to a series.

Pivots in tires are common show obstacles. You'll need a great deal of control here. Sometimes, a course will call for a complete 360-degree pivot or a pivot half-way around. Some will test you by having the horse do a turn on the forehand with his front feet in, then walk through until the back feet are in the tire, and do a turn on the haunches. Patient schooling is required at home and you should NEVER attempt these obstacles until your horse has been taught the turns on the forehand and haunches AWAY from the obstacle, and has had his "single-tire" schooling.

7.13. Push his sides with your hand and ask him to move away from the pressure. Ask for only one or two steps at first.

7.14. Gradually ask him to turn more with each session.

Start with a medium-sized tire, though you will probably be asked to pivot in a large tractor tire, when you do the obstacle at a show. You must be prepared for anything since you never really know which size they'll ask you to pivot in. When you start the schooling, however, you should not use a tire that's too big to worry the horse, nor so small-centered that his feet have no room to move. The ideal pivot is one in which the horse plants his pivot feet in the tire and keeps them still. The green horse is going to move his feet some at first, until he gets the idea, so he needs the room to do so.

First, teach the horse to pivot with his front feet in. This is a turn on the forehand. Lead him up and have him step in the tire with his front feet. Stand him there and let him relax. After a few minutes, place your fingers on his side in the same area your heels would be if you were aboard. When he moves his hindquarters away from the pressure, move your hand away from him. Even if you only get one step, he's getting the idea and it's time to stop. Pet him, let him stand, then ask for another step. Be sure you're steadying his head, should

7.15. When riding, walk him into the tire. Take hold of his head to restrict him from walking out.

7.16. As you steady his head, leg him to push his hindquarters away from your leg and around the tire. This horse is being pushed off the left leg and the right one is staying out of him to avoid contradiction of aids.

7.17. Ride FORWARD out of the tire after a pivot! Never try to back out, or the horse will get a foot hung up. This is also the way to get the back feet placed in the tire for a turn on the haunches. Ride THROUGH the tire and stop the horse when his back feet are in. When you are through with the pivot, ride forward—don't back out.

he try to walk out of the tire. Keep his front end in, get two steps, then quit for that session. When you're done, NEVER BACK HIM OUT OF THE TIRE. Always walk him out straight so he doesn't get hung up.

After a few days, bring the horse back and work him on the obstacle. Place his feet in and push his sides. You need to spend several days, or weeks if necessary, getting him to accept the pressure of your hand and move away from it until he is making a full turn around the tire, pivoting off his front feet. Some horses learn this very quickly. Others continue to try and step out, or try to do it quickly. The ideal situation with the "quick" horse is to ask him to take one step, stop him for a few minutes, then take another step, stop him—repeating this until he accepts the fact that he is to do it slowly and carefully. If your horse just rushes around the tire in his pivot while being shown, the judge will knock him down for it. While he wants to see the job get done without the horse and rider poking, he wants to see it done *carefully*. If you stop and start the horse at home, when you then take him all the way around the tire *without* stopping, he's going to do it ever so carefully. He'll be waiting for your cue for every step, expecting to stop. This will give him some caution and keep him from flying around carelessly.

When you're ready to ride your horse up to the tire, do so with the same method you led him through. Start by quietly riding him up, placing his feet in the tire, then standing him there. You'll need to repeat the "one-step-at-a-time" schooling. Remember—in a turn on the forehand, you hold his head in place with your hands, restricting him from walking out of the tire. You leg him with your calf and heel to move his body over. Sit up straight in the saddle so that he can move without interference. And, remember—RIDE OUT THROUGH THE TIRE, DON'T BACK OUT, or the horse might get hung up on the tire rim.

Schooling the horse to do a pivot with his back feet in the tire is merely working a turn on the haunches. You may have to manually place the back feet in the tire. First, try leading the horse through slowly, stepping his front feet in the center as he would do normally when walking through a tire. When his first back foot is in, tell him "whoa" and hold him there a few moments so he knows he's not to walk through. Gently coax his other back foot into the center, then stop him and stand there a LONG time. He's used to following his front feet with his back just "leaving" the tire, and hasn't had the concept of standing with his back feet in introduced to him yet. If he starts to move out and steps on the rim, you can back him a little to replace his foot. He won't be likely to hang up a foot on the rim if he's coming out forward.

For the horse who doesn't get the idea of stepping in himself, walk him through with his front feet, then stop him. He'll be standing, hopefully quietly, with his front feet on one side of the tire, and his back feet on the other. Manually place one back foot in the tire and hold him there for a while. Then, go around and place the other foot in. If he respects the word "whoa" and has had all the basic single-tire schooling, he won't be as likely to try to step one foot out while you go around for the other one.

When the horse is standing quietly with both back feet in the tire, take your reins and *gently* push his head away from you and ask him for ONE step with his front feet. This is when he might try to step out of the tire, so you must be sure to hold him in and keep him from stepping all the way out. If he moves a foot on the rim, back him in and tell him "WHOA." Try again to "rein" his head so he takes one step. Often, pushing against his shoulder with your hand helps him understand. This is another instance where you MUST only ask for a step or two at a time and spend days or weeks building up to a complete turn. Your horse's reaction will tell you how long it's going to take. If he's nervous and doesn't get the idea, you need to spend a lot of time "holding" him in the tire, getting him to relax. Try spending several days just making him stand with his back feet in *without* asking him for a turn. When he's confident, get one or two steps out of him, or any minor beginning of a pivot, and quit. TAKE YOUR TIME!

Don't try riding your horse on this obstacle until he's thoroughly schooled on the ground-work portion of it. When he's ready to be ridden on the obstacle, ride him into the tire and through, being sure he goes through as he should with his front feet. Stop him when his back feet are in, and position him so those feet are in dead center of the tire. Let's look at a turn to the right to explain your aids. You'll have contact with your horse's mouth, using your hands to keep him from

7.18. When teaching the "back-feet-in" pivot from the ground, position the horse as shown and manually place his back feet in the tire. Most green horses will try to evade the tire with their back feet if you lead them through it. This way works best at first, until they get the idea.

7.19. Push against the shoulder and move the horse's head and front end around.

walking out forward. As you lightly rein him to the right, you use light leg pressure with your LEFT leg to push his front end around. You might help him by using your leg pressure a ways ahead of the usual position you use when you're asking him to move his hindquarters away from you—closer to the cinch. You can change your leg position *without* altering your body position. You shouldn't be moving your body at all. As you "push" the horse around with your left leg and rein him with your hand, you'll be applying gentle leg pressure (milder than the left leg) on the right side, which keeps his body in a straight line and doesn't allow him to overbend into the direction of the pivot.

A turn on the haunches, whether it be out in the open or in a tire, is done with the same principles as a stock-horse turn. Let's look at the way a stock horse does a half or full turn. He rocks back on his hindquarters with the heaviest weight on his inside leg or pivot foot. His body remains relatively straight, and his front legs "swing" around as his front end "rotates," while he remains planted on the pivot foot. Though this horse is definitely broke and supple and could bend into his turn if asked, he's been brought along to the point of keeping his body straight as he turns—not bending his neck and head into that direction. This is how your pivot in the tire should look—no overbending. There should be a great deal of control shown and a lot of controlled movement. The horse should be collected up and moving in balance with the same basic moves as a stock horse. Your horse will be doing it in "slow motion."

Remember to WALK OUT THROUGH THE TIRE, and not back out. Don't get your horse hung up, or have him so off center during the turn that he bumps his legs against the rim and hurts himself. Anytime a horse gets hurt on an obstacle, it destroys the confidence and trust you're working so hard to instill.

Always remember, when working tires in the show ring, that the judge is looking for a horse that "feels" with his feet and tries to hit that tire dead center. He should go like he's "walking on eggs" and he shouldn't cheat. If your horse has been fully schooled on tires and later becomes lazy, stepping on the rims and not watching where he's going, get right back to single-tire schooling, backing him off each time he steps on a rim. If he tries to cheat and duck off to the side, and leg pressure won't straighten him out, set your single tire between two telephone poles, large posts or logs, or two bales of hay. Gradually build him back up to a row with this side restriction. When he sees this side restriction, he'll think twice before trying to step out, and you can bet he'll stop cheating!

7.20. *This type of obstacle is good to use when schooling a* finished *horse that has become lazy and tries to walk to the outside of a tire* row.

7.21. *A look at a more finished horse in a pivot. Wendy Daniels does a turn on the haunches with Candy Bar.*

Remember your part in "riding tires":

1. When approaching a row, give the horse his head several feet before, so he can pace himself. Often a horse will miss a tire because he hasn't had this proper start.

2. Sit still right in the center of the horse. Your cue for him to walk over will be to lean forward in the saddle, and release his head. This is done without a "big move." It is done quietly with your upper, not your lower, body changing. Don't shift off to the side!

3. Keep your position until your horse has come off the

7.22. *Wendy is asking Candy for a turn on the forehand. See how the mare crosses her back feet in the movement. She is going to Wendy's right. The left leg is pushing her off, the right leg is out away from her side. Wendy steadies her head to keep her front end in place.*

last tire. If you sit up before he is completely through, he'll flub the last tire with his back feet.

4. When doing your pivots, pay close attention to your body movements. Try not to make any! If you need to look behind you to see where the back feet are, move your head, but not your entire body. If you MUST lean, do it when the horse is standing still before he's started to pivot . . . NOT while he's moving.

Give your horse every chance to be a top performer on tires. Patient schooling and "using your head" with every move will produce a winner!

7.23. An advanced tire obstacle built by Wendy's father consists of a box with divider slats, plastic tarp on the bottom, and four tires. It can be filled with water for a tricky water tire obstacle.

Chapter Eight

Backthroughs and Backarounds

Most of the problems arising in working on backthroughs and backaround obstacles stem from trying to work them too fast, or from working the horse on too difficult obstacles before he's ready. A horse naturally needs all the basics, taught *away* from the obstacles, before he's asked to work a backup.

If you study the photos of Wendy and Candy Bar in this chapter, you can see there is very little reins "stress" regardless of which type of backup the mare is working. This type of response is a definite plus in a trail horse. All Wendy has to do to bring the mare back is close her bottom fingers on the reins. The mare will feel it and respond. Not all horses will do this. It's something you work on and develop, doing the best you can.

Before a horse ever works any type of backup, whether it be an L-shaped backthrough or cloverleaf barrels, he must also be thoroughly schooled on turns on the forehand and haunches. You should be able to gently rein his front end into any position you wish—move any foot anyplace, anytime. If a horse knows ALL the basics, you should be able to do a

146

pretty good job of working a simple backthrough the first time you try it.

START WITH STRAIGHT BACKTHROUGHS

Telephone poles, large logs, or railroad ties make the best backthroughs for schooling a green horse. Why? You don't want him to step easily over and out of a backthrough, or to learn that if he touches it slightly, it's going to roll out of his way. The purpose of schooling him is to teach him to perform the backthrough without touching the obstacle at all. Since the judge will someday be watching closely, scoring you on how carefully the horse works, you have to school your horse from the beginning to be cautious.

There are two trains of thought on how to space backthroughs for a green horse. The general feeling is that a green horse travels wide with his feet until he learns to "scrunch in" and travel narrow. For this reason, some trainers start with a widely spaced backup and teach the horse to travel narrow *gradually* by closing the space in a little with each session. Other trainers want their horses traveling narrow from the start and begin with about 24 inches of space for the horse to move in. So much depends on the horse. Some are more athletic than others and can work in a tight spot easily. Others need work on coordination. Take a close look at what YOUR horse needs. If he's athletic, space your poles 24 inches apart. If you feel he needs a gradual increase in difficulty, give him as much as 36 inches to work in.

When you have your straight backthrough set up, using poles, logs, or railroad ties, you might want to introduce the horse to the concept by working from the ground at first. Walk WITH your horse and lead him forward into the backthrough. This gives him a chance to "see where he is." When his front legs are out, but his back still in, stop and relax him. Stand there a few moments, then, while still standing in front of

8.1. *Telephone poles or railroad ties are best for backthroughs in the beginning, but with the more finished Candy Bar, Wendy is schooling on heavy raised poles. Here, she is riding Candy forward into the backthrough, altering the usual situation to keep Candy careful.*

8.2. *After the front legs cleared, the mare was stopped and backed through the obstacle.*

8.3. *She must be kept straight throughout.*

him, ask him to back quietly two or three steps, then stop again. (We like to school our horses to back on command and stop on "whoa." This way we can maintain a loose lead shank or rein and move them on voice alone during the ground-work.) When the horse has been standing quietly for a few moments, move him back two or three more steps, then stop him. What you're trying to instill is the ability of the horse to RELAX and work the backthrough as you command him. Some horses, hauled back too quickly, learn to think back-throughs are "race-throughs" that they can do quickly at their own pace. Your horse has to be taught to *creep* through this backup, waiting for you to tell him when and how.

When you reach the end of the backthrough, be sure to slowly (with the "stop-start" method) back your horse a few feet straight out. If you don't, he'll learn to cheat and will start to turn and move off in a crooked manner each time he thinks he's out of the poles.

When the horse has had one or two sessions being led through the backthrough, ride him into it just as you led him into it. Stand him quietly at the front with his hind legs still in between the poles. Take a light hold of him and ask him to back two or three steps, then tell him "whoa." Stand there five minutes or more if you feel he's a little anxious. Teach him there's no reason why he can't stand quietly in this ob-stacle. He needs to learn that nobody's rushing him. Back him out slowly with several pauses, being sure to back him straight out a few feet, then stop him.

To keep a horse from becoming bored, you should change your backthrough by moving it as often as possible. Also, ride in from the other side once in a while. Don't enter the same way, at the same place each session or he IS going to start backing it out of habit alone. Once in a while, approach the poles from the side and work them as a stepover.

Teaching the Trail Horse to Work an "L"

When you set up your first L-shaped backthrough, you should use the same heavy materials as the original straight backthrough. A green trail horse will have to learn to "feel" for the corner, and in doing so, he may be inclined to step out over the edge. If you use the proper materials, he won't be able to step out and he'll learn to feel a lot faster!

Keep your spacing wide enough in the L that the horse has room to maneuver. Even though he might have been working a 24-inch straight backthrough, he'll propably need a wider L at first. He's going to be asked to do more in this obstacle, and he'll need the extra room.

Ride your horse into the L, riding him around the corner and to the front opening just as you did with the straight backthrough. This gives him a look at the corner and an idea of what he'll be asked to do.

Ride him up until the horse's front legs are out, but his hind legs are still in. This keeps him "trapped" so he doesn't turn and get away from the obstacle. Now, as you start to work the horse on an L, you'll need to pay close attention to your "equitation" to help your horse instead of hinder him.

The best way to avoid trouble, both in working the L for schooling, and working it in front of a judge, is to be sure you're spaced properly before you start. Your horse should be right in the center of the two poles. He shouldn't be closer to one than the other. If he is, he's going to travel off to one side and hit the L. If you start him right out in proper position, you don't have to spend as much time looking to see where you are. You'll only have to watch ONE side. The biggest mistake made by novice trail horse riders is looking from one side to the other, leaning way out of the saddle, "rocking" the horse as he's trying to move back in a straight line. More horses hit a pole from rider mistakes than from their own.

8.4. *The most important part of successfully backing an L is the beginning positioning. Wendy positions Candy so her back feet are evenly spaced in the opening.*

8.5. *After clearing the corner, Candy's back legs are moved over.*

8.6. *Her front end was reined around, and she was slowly backed out.*

Now, if you're positioned correctly, you should only have to watch the inside corner of the L. Let's say you're backing and will turn to the right (the horse's rear end will turn right in the first move). All you should have to do is remain straight in the saddle and look down with your eyes—NOT your whole body—at the right side of the backthrough. If you're not too close to that pole, you can judge your position from the center. If you're a long ways from it, you can bet you'll hit the left side. If you KNOW you were centered perfectly in the beginning, you work to KEEP there.

Back your horse one step at a time, stopping momentarily between each step. It is more beneficial to spend twenty minutes working an L ONCE, correctly, than it is to run through it a dozen times. "Inch" back, step by step. As soon as the horse's back legs step just behind the inside corner of the turn, stop and hold him there. You'll want to get both your bearings, because at this point he's going to do something

8.A. Methods for lining up for a backthrough.

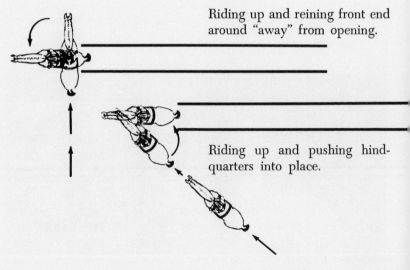

Riding up and reining front end around "away" from opening.

Riding up and pushing hind-quarters into place.

different—turning while backing. Take a light hold on his head, and use your "outside" leg to gently and slowly move his hindquarters around into the turn. Ask for one step at a time in between. As soon as his back legs are in position and have made the turn, STOP and hold him a few moments; then rein his front end around to straighten him out, and STOP him again. The greatest schooling you can do at this point is to hold the horse here for as long as ten minutes. It takes patience to make a trail horse! Many trail horses who have been schooled improperly, think that when the turn is made, it's a run for your money and a chance to "fly" out of the backthrough. You want to properly school your horse so he leaves the L as slowly and carefully as he entered it.

You may want to spend several weeks riding your horse into the L and backing him out. Be sure to approach it differently, alternating between left and right turns, so he doesn't become a one-way horse.

Once your horse gets the idea of how to back and turn in close quarters, you can begin thinking about setting up varied types of backthroughs. Whenever possible, ride him into them until you feel he's ready to learn to approach it in a more finished manner. Trying for an approach too soon often causes a horse to blow up at the obstacle.

TEACHING THE APPROACH

Two of the easiest ways to line a horse up for a backthrough are shown in the diagram on page 152. The first way consists of riding the horse up to where one pole is coming "in from the side" right about at his front legs, and the other pole the same way at his back legs. When a horse is standing this way, all you need do is rein his front end around (away from the entrance) until he becomes parallel to the poles. This approach should place his back feet right in the center and ready to back.

The other way is simply to ride up in a somewhat parallel position, clear the poles with the horse's back feet, and hold his front end still while you push his back end around to make him parallel to the poles. This should be done with great care so that when he's straight, he's RIGHT at the opening and not two or three feet away from it.

If you have any trouble getting your horse to approach properly, you can try it from the ground. For the first approach, lead the horse up and stop him, then lead him slowly around to get him in a parallel position. For the second approach, come up on the side and position him by stopping him, then push his hindquarters over by pushing lightly with your hand at his side. Whichever you choose, first hold him there, then stand in front and ask him to back at least part way into the obstacle.

BACKING BARRELS

In the show ring, you may be asked to back around barrels or poles, or other types of markers. You can't back a "bunch"

8.7. *Getting a horse accustomed to "barrel-rocking" is an important part of schooling him to accept those noisy barrels.*

8.8. *Pushing the barrel over teaches the horse to accept its falling and not panic.*

without teaching the horse on a single one first. Let's look at the concept of backing barrels.

Many horses panic if a barrel tips over, or if they hear the rider's stirrup or foot hit it. While you don't want a horse to work the obstacle carelessly, you don't want him to think he's going to get in trouble if a barrel tips over. You also want to instill some confidence in him, so he won't be afraid of the sound of a barrel crashing over. The best way to do this is to ride up alongside a barrel and stand the horse quietly. Teach him to relax!

When he's quiet, remove your foot from the stirrup, rock the barrel with your foot, and ask the horse to stand and accept it. If he seems nervous, spend several sessions just standing and rocking the barrel a little. When he's calm, push the barrel over and ask him to stand quietly.

You start backing barrels with a single barrel. Begin with the horse's hindquarters aimed towards the barrel, straight away from it, a few feet out. Keep in mind that here you'll actually be turning rather than backing. You DON'T have to

8.B. Cloverleaf barrel pattern.

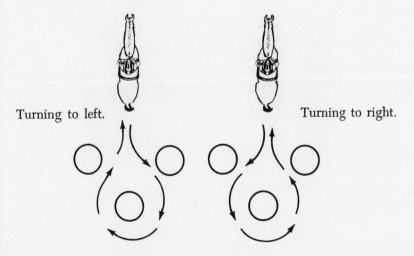

Turning to left.   Turning to right.

8.9. *The important thing in backing a single barrel is to keep the hindquarters close and move the front end around.*

8.10. *Here, Wendy has legged Candy to the left, keeping the hindquarters in and swinging the front end out away. It's actually more turning than backing.*

8.11. *Wendy backs the mare straight away from the single barrel. If it were one of three in the cloverleaf, she would again swing the mare's hindquarters in and move the front end away.*

keep the horse's front end close to the barrel. You should actually be keeping his rear end close to it, moving his front end away and around.

Study the photos of Wendy backing the single barrel on Candy on page 156. She begins by backing fairly straight to the right side of the barrel. She's careful not to knock the barrel over with her foot. As she begins to go around the barrel, she "hugs" it with Candy's hindquarters, and moves her front end away from it. After rounding it, she backs right away. If she were working a cloverleaf pattern, she should, again, get the mare's hindquarters close to the barrel and move the front end away to back out between the other barrels.

It's best to spend a great deal of time—not in one session however—working your horse around a single barrel or pole. The top trail horse trainers seem to spend "forever and a day" on basics to gain a horse's confidence. Then, when they move on to more difficult steps, they do it in small degrees, spacing obstacles so the horse will have it fairly easy until he gets the idea. In the photos of Wendy working a cloverleaf pattern with three barrels on page 158, you can see that the spacing is fairly tight. Having set up the barrels myself, I can attest to the fact. For a green horse, however, the spacing should be much farther apart. He won't feel "trapped" or scare himself by moving wrong and backing into a barrel.

Don't try the cloverleaf pattern until your horse is ready. When you do try it, space it widely, and gradually work it into the spacing Wendy is using. Let's study how the cloverleaf is done.

In the show ring, the judge will tell you which way he wants you to turn in the cloverleaf pattern. In the photos on page 158, Wendy is working it on a left-turn basis. She lines up, stops and gets her bearings. Candy is then backed between the two barrels on the *right*. Her rear end is kept close to the

8.12. *The cloverleaf pattern consists of three barrels. Wendy lines the mare up to begin.*

8.13. *Going between the two barrels, Wendy gets into position to back around.*

8.14. *The hindquarters are kept close in to the barrel, and the front end is carefully reined around.*

8.15. *Now, she'll move the hindquarters into the opening between the two barrels on the left of the picture.*

8.16. Notice how she raises her leg to clear the barrel. If a rider knocks it down, it's as bad for the score as if the horse did it.

8.17. Wendy backs Candy out of the obstacle to complete it.

"inside" barrel—the one she is to back around. As she clears, her hindquarters are still close to the barrel, and her front end is reined away. In positioning to back out, Wendy has to move the mare's back end closer in, and back out between the two barrels on the left. NOTICE HOW, WHEN WORKING CLOSE TO A BARREL, WENDY RAISES HER FOOT UP TO CLEAR IT! A rider knocking down a barrel loses as many points as a horse does. Candy Bar is 14.2 hands, and the barrels seem large next to her, as compared to a larger horse. Wendy has to reach high to clear the barrel when working it close.

COMBINATIONS

It's impossible to duplicate all the combinations of obstacles that you'll see in the show ring. You never know what you'll have to work until you enter the class and see the course posted. It's important that you vary your schooling a great deal at home to prepare your horse for anything. Look at the "U"-shaped backthrough in which Barbara is riding the Pinto

8.18. *This type of schooling backthrough has two turns and helps fight the "L syndrome" in horses—their thinking that after the first turn, it's time to back straight out.*

mare (photo above). This has *two* corners. You can school your horse on it for a second turn, keeping him out of the "L syndrome"—his thinking that he's completed the obstacle after rounding the first turn. This obstacle was made from a "little bit of everything" and nailed in place to make it heavy.

8.19. *This backthrough was made of "a little bit of everything" nailed in place to keep it stout and heavy.*

After initial telephone-pole or railroad-tie schooling, you can go on to such things as the elevated jump poles that Wendy schools Candy on (see below). Her father made them from 4×4 or larger posts (depending on how heavy a pole they wanted) and shearing (planing off) the edges.

8.20. Wendy schools on this combination because it's a great one for helping a horse and rider learn to work together carefully and slowly.

8.21. After the back feet are out of the poles, but the front still in, Wendy legs Candy over to the side of the barrel.

8.22, 8.23. *She turns the mare carefully around the barrel.*

8.24. *Returning to the backthrough, they back quietly out of the poles. Notice the light contact with the mouth and the "softness" of Wendy's hand on the reins.*

In the photos preceding, Wendy is schooling Candy on a combination of backthrough and barrel. She backs Candy slowly out the backthrough, starting to turn her hindquarters before her front legs are out. She rounds the barrel, then returns to the backthrough to back slowly out of the poles. These obstacles are terrific for getting the horse and rider to work together, teaching them that you can't be in a hurry if you want to be successful in show ring backthroughs!

Chapter Nine

Jumps and Half-Jumps

Teaching a trail horse to jump is very much like schooling a hunter. You're after the same basics. A trail horse must also tuck his legs, use his head and neck well, and be able to maneuver an in-and-out if the two-jump obstacle is put before him. While judges might have been lenient on the way horses jumped in the past, trail-horse judges today want to see them jump like hunters.

The best way to introduce a trail horse to jumping is to longe him over them. You'll need a sturdy jump that he can't knock over with a slight hit; yet you don't want to put too big a jump at him in the beginning, or you'll lose the chance of building confidence in him. One of the best jumps to start a horse on is one similar to the "tire-and-log" jump shown in the pictures (see p. 167). You can use a log or regular jump pole, or, if you don't have either, a long 4×4 post. A 2×4 would be too flimsy and knock over too easily. It might even split if the horse hit it just right.

Place two stacked tires on each end of the pole. The weight of the pole causes the tires to "squish" a little. To help discourage the horse from running out, set the jump up against a fence so the fence is on one side and YOU are on the other. You might also add a wing to your side of the jump which is merely another pole lying parallel to the fence. The fence and the wing help to "funnel" the horse directly into the center of the jump.

When you position yourself to longe your horse over a jump, you do so by a method that makes the diameter of the horse's circle fall in line with the jump pole. If you have the advantage of holding a longeing whip, your hand controls the horse's head and your whip is aimed at his hindquarters. You're actually "holding" the horse between your hand and your whip. The fence holds him on one side, the wing on the other, and YOU keep him going. His chances for evading the jump are few.

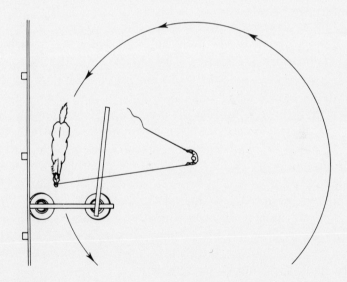

9.A. To longe a horse over a jump, place the horse along an arena wall and use a pole as a wing on the side (parallel to the horse as shown). Position yourself so that the diameter of the horse's circle falls in line with the jump pole. Use a whip to hold the horse between your left hand, with the longe line, and your right hand, with the whip.

Longe your horse in a circle for a few laps a little ways away from the jump and gradually move him so that he has to take the jump. Don't jump him time and time again. Make him jump it once or twice, then move him back so he can make two or three circles away from it. Too much consistent jumping will cause a horse to become sour. Try working him mostly from the trot and be sure to work him BOTH ways. Many horses are easier to longe in one direction and their handlers will only longe them that way. A horse jumped from one direction will become so one-way that he will lock up if he ever has to work in the other direction. A trail horse needs flexible schooling to be flexible—to work any obstacle from any position at any time.

Spend at least several days teaching your horse to jump a simple pole jump. Later, if he has the ability and is willing, you should start on more of a spread. A horse that learns to jump *wide* before he learns to jump *high* builds ability and confidence at the same time. Set up a second jump, parallel to the first. Start by placing it about three feet from the first and gradually increase the spread. You're trying to get your horse to tuck his front legs up and under him, and to lift and tuck his hind legs. Some horses will clear with the front and hit with the back, so you have to school on these spreads to teach your horse to USE his body correctly. When he's working well on spreads, THEN you can give him more height. Longe him over a row of hay bales, barrels, or stacked railroad ties. Try to get him confident enough to jump anything "strange" that you put before him.

When you begin teaching the horse to work a LEADOVER jump, try to get someone to help you. Set up the same basic jump you used when you started jumping the horse on the longe. You're going to teach him the "stop-stand-come-over" method because it's the most widely used system in today's shows. Let's examine the WHY before we examine the how.

Over the years, trail horses were asked to perform on jumps where, in most cases, the rider dismounted and tried to trot over a jump with the horse. Several things can go wrong in this situation. If the rider tries to run up and get over the jump either at the same time, or just before the horse jumps, one of these mishaps is bound to occur:

1. The handler is going to inadvertently jerk down on the reins since it is nearly impossible to give a horse a loose rein and perform this way.

2. A rider might trip over his own chap fringe by stepping on the fringe of one leg with the opposite foot. It's easy to fall in this case.

3. It's not easy to maneuver when you're wearing tight chaps! If you try to "run, then leap" at this jump, you're

9.1. In teaching the leadover jump, lead the horse up and stop him, making him stand several minutes.

9.2. *Give him the command to stand or stay while you step over the jump. Don't let him come over until YOU want him to.*

9.3. *Without restricting his head, or standing directly in front of him, cluck to him as you move off, and bring him over the jump.*

probably going to knock the pole down. If a rider knocks over an obstacle, it will cost as many points as if the horse does it, as the obstacle has not been worked successfully.

4. Picture yourself, wearing a pair of spurs, jumping over a pole, kicking your leg up high behind you. Guess where that puts your spur!

Running up on a jump and trying to take it the same time as your horse does just doesn't give you enough time to "get it all together" and in most cases, it will look like it is—a mess. This is why the system of jumping your horse from a standstill AFTER you're over is so successful. Here's how you teach it.

Put some type of control device on your horse's head. Put his lead rope through the halter under his chin. Use a chain shank, or some type of rope war bridle, if you think your horse will need it. What you want is to teach your horse to respond to both your voice and what you do with his head. You'll probably need someone behind the horse at first to coax him over, but remember that this should be temporary. He has to learn to jump when you, the person at the end of his lead rope, ask him to do it.

Lead your horse up to the jump, about a foot or two in front of it. Stand quietly with him, as Barbara is doing in the photos with Dusty on page 167. Tell your horse to "stand" or "stay" as you step over the jump. You may, at first, have to reach back with your shank hand and push him back a little to enforce the verbal command. Make him stand there quietly until you're ready to bring him over. Stand out of his way, but not so much to the side that he'll be encouraged to run out. Give him enough loose lead shank that you won't jerk on his head and cluck to him or tell him to "come on" as you walk off. He should come over. If he doesn't, have someone behind him tap him with a whip. If you're by yourself, you might try a hard tug down on the shank which will set him back a couple

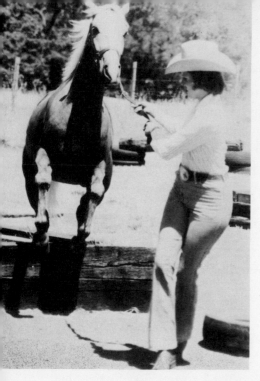

9.4. *Dusty is tucking his front legs fairly well for a green horse, while Barbara brings him over two railroad ties.*

9.5. *Willingly jumping a* bridge, *Dusty exhibits how a well-schooled, confident horse will "follow you anywhere."*

of steps, then encourage him to come over when you repeat the signals. After he comes over, keep walking off with him. There will be jumps in the show ring where you have to stop a horse immediately after going over, but if you try to teach a horse to stop too soon in his schooling, he won't jump as well. Rather than worrying about tucking his legs and getting over correctly, he'll be worried about stopping, and it will cramp his style!

Practice this type of leadover jump on several different obstacles so the horse will come over anything you put before him. When he's leading over well, try jumping him over something while you step out on the side *just in case* you might be asked to do this type of jump someday in the show ring. The photos on page 170 show Barbara leading Dusty over two stacked railroad ties. This front shot shows you how this green horse is learning to tuck his front legs. In the next photo, Barbara is leading the horse on a jump which consists of a *bridge* which is high *and wide*. Here she's off to the side. This shows that a properly started horse will come over anything put in front of him because he's obedient and has confidence in the handler. Take special notice in these pictures that Barbara has contact with the horse through the shank but is NOT jerking on his head. There is a reasonable amount of slack at all times.

"Saddling-up" for Leadover Jumps

Practice your leadover jumps at home with the horse saddled, by riding up, dismounting, performing the jump, then mounting and riding off as if you were going to the next obstacle. The photos on page 173 show the method of handling romel reins in the dismount and mount. The system is basically the same as with split reins. All you would adjust is the handling of your split reins as opposed to the romel.

Ride up so that you are a few feet from the jump. Don't

crowd it. Remember that you are trying to show CON-TROLLED and CAREFUL movement, so you do this slowly, paying attention to each step. Don't think just darting off your horse and pulling the reins over his head will impress a judge, because it won't! You have to do everything smoothly.

Study the photos following. Before Barbara dismounts, she passes the romel from her right hand to her left. See how it's doubled so there is a "loop" above the grip of her left hand? From here, she dismounts by placing her right hand on the horn and swinging her right leg over the horse's rump, being careful not to kick the mare with her right foot. All this time, the reins have contact with the horse's mouth. She doesn't toss the mare's head away, or the horse might walk off. A good trail horse stands completely still and is very quiet while a rider dismounts. In your home-schooling, use a firm "WHOA" to stop the horse if he tries to move.

9.6. When riding up to a leadover jump, stop the horse and do a proper dismount.

9.7. *Get your reins properly positioned and "get everything together" before starting over.*

9.8. *Make the horse stand while you step over.*

9.9. *When both you and the horse are in position, cue him to jump from a standstill. Stay out of his way and don't jerk his head!*

9.10. Your horse should be schooled to stand quietly while you mount. Proper *mounting procedures will encourage your horse to remain still.*

9.11. After your reins are in position, your feet placed in the stirrups and everything is "together," THEN you can ride off to the next obstacle.

After slowly taking the reins over the horse's head, Barbara "gets organized" by taking the romel in her left hand and the reins in her right. She then tells the mare to stand, after leading her up a little closer to the jump. Barbara slowly steps over the pole, being careful not to pull on the mare's head, a mistake which would cause a premature jump. After she's over and is "together" enough to ask the mare to jump, she clucks to her as she begins to walk away. She's out of the way, so the horse can come over. She is NOT hanging on the head or jerking the mare's mouth. In these jumps, the rider must get out in front a little so the horse does not jump PAST the handler. This would cause a jerk on the mouth.

Near the jump, Barbara prepares to remount. This must be

correctly done and carefully controlled. The reins have been put back over the head and the rein and romel are again in the left hand. It's permissible to place your left hand on the horse's neck just ahead of the withers to help brace yourself when mounting. If you have a horse that's "mutton-withered" and doesn't hold a saddle well, bracing your left hand a little on the neck might help you avoid rolling the saddle.

Barbara, in the photo on page 174, has her reins short enough to discourage the horse from walking off. A trail horse MUST stand while the rider mounts. If you mount correctly, the horse won't be "pushed away" from you. Twist your stirrup with your right hand to put it in position to place your left foot well in. Keep your body erect and close to your horse. Take hold of the horn with your right hand, and gracefully raise yourself up, NOT leaning over the horse. Swing your leg over, being careful not to bump your horse, then position yourself in the saddle. Keep the horse standing quietly as you pass the romel back to your left hand. Don't cue your horse to walk off until you have everything "together" and are *ready*.

RIDEOVER JUMPS

The most important thing to remember in rideover jumps is that your horse has to KNOW for sure before he gets up to it that it's a jump and not a stepover. The cue for a stepover is the leaning forward of the rider and the lowering of the horse's head. When you want him to jump, you need a separate cue. You should sit TALL, pick his head up a little and cluck to him. The impulsion of the jump will boost you forward a little as the horse jumps, but you should sit straight up in the saddle during the approach and try not to lean so far over him during the jump that you're "laying on his neck." During all rideover jumps, you should have some contact with his mouth if you need it, but should never have a hard, restrictive hold on the horse. You should square your lower body completely, sitting

9.12. *This barrel jump is good for practice, particularly in schooling a horse to tuck his legs. Notice how Barbara is staying balanced in the saddle, even though her upper body is a little off to the left. Her stirrups are even as her weight is evenly distributed in them.*

9.13. *A regular pole jump with standards is best for starting a green horse on jumps with a rider aboard.*

down in the saddle as the horse approaches. If you have any reason to look to the side as the horse jumps, lean only with your head and shoulders and NOT move your lower body. This point is best illustrated in the photo on page 176 of Barbara jumping Good News over the barrel jump. Barbara's feet are even. The stirrups are the same length, showing that she is square in the saddle and has equal pressure coming down through her heels. Her upper body is slightly off to the side, but it has NOT affected her lower body position. The mare's head is free, and she's jumping well, tucking her front legs.

A regular hunter-jumper type set-up, such as the pole and standards shown on page 176, is the best one for teaching a horse to jump with a rider aboard. This is a wide jump, giving the horse plenty of room to get over; the standards on the side discourage him from running out. Ideally, the horse should go right over the center of the jump. This is done by positioning him a few yards from the jump and approaching straight and true, right for the center. At first, you might try jogging up to get the horse in the "moving mood," so he's less likely to stop. Several feet before the jump, squeeze lightly with your legs, sit up tall and cluck to him. If he's been taught to jump on the longe line, you should have little trouble getting him to jump the first time you try to ride him over. When you get over the jump, keep him in a straight line, moving away from the jump. Don't teach him to stop until he is completely schooled on jumping "like a hunter"—tucking his legs and moving freely over the jump. Later, you can school him to jump from the walk, and go on to teach him to jump from the lope.

Set up two jumps, parallel to one another, to teach the horse to handle ins-and-outs. Initially there should be enough distance that the horse can come down off the first one, take two strides, then jump out the second. It has to be EASY at first, adjusted to his own, particular length of stride. After *many* lessons at a simple in-and-out, start to close it up, so he only has one stride in between. Eventually, you'll want him clever enough to land, gather up, and spring off all in a very small distance.

One good obstacle to school on is the three-sided jump, made of poles set on car tires, shown in the photos below. This can be used in a variety of ways. First Barbara is shown entering the jump by bringing the mare in from the right side. She then uses it as a simple in-and-out by taking the mare right out over the parallel pole. Another way to school is to jump in and stop the horse long enough to turn to the left and then jump out. You can do it a little differently each time.

STOPPING AFTER A JUMP

The reasons for not teaching a horse to stop too soon in his schooling have already been touched on. If he's expecting to stop all the time, he's not going to "jump like a hunter." The best way to teach a horse to stop is to do it VERY SELDOM

9.14. *This three-sided jump is good for schooling. Here, Barbara jumps the mare in.*

9.15. *After one stride, the mare is jumped out.*

9.16. The obstacle is versatile in that you can use it several ways. Here, the mare is entered from the right, turned, and brought out to the left of the entrance point.

and to simply be assured that he understands the word "WHOA" and will react to it immediately. Occasionally, set a pole down on the ground after the jump, such as the one Barbara is holding the mare behind after taking her over the jump with standards. WHEN you ask for the stop is going to affect just how good the jump is. If you don't wait until the *back legs clear* before giving the command "WHOA," the horse is going to stop too soon, and grab for the ground with his back legs. He'll hit them against the pole, and your jump will be a total loss. Use timing. As soon as you feel the back legs are clear of the jump and have come over, tell the horse "WHOA." Don't "jerk his head off." If you have to, take hold of him lightly, but don't jerk on him. If you do, his head will fly up and you'll get a bad stop.

At first, give him plenty of room to stop. Gradually, you can ask him to stop in a shorter space. Just remember to SELDOM work on this, so your horse won't anticipate the stop. If you're having a real problem with him, and the pole on the ground doesn't work, set your jump up parallel to an arena fence, far enough away that it won't discourage him from jumping, but

9.17. *Placing a ground pole parallel to the jump is an aid in teaching a horse to stop immediately after jumping.*

close enough that he will be head on to the fence if he tries to evade the word "whoa." When you're schooling, always make your horse stand quietly for several minutes after the jump. You don't ever want a trail horse to think he can walk off any time *he* thinks he's finished with a job.

HALF-JUMPS

Half-jumps are common in the show ring in the classes for finished horses. In general, green classes won't have them. They are somewhat tricky because they're not usually very high, and a horse might try to step rather than jump over them. A half-jump is just that—the "front half" of the horse jumps over, then the jump is stopped while the back legs are still on the "other" side of the jump. What generally happens is that a horse half-jumps over an obstacle and sidepasses off. You can see in the photos of Barbara taking the mare over the tire-and-log jump on page 181 that the mare is stopping more on verbal command than on rein pressure. Barbara has jumped her front end over, then told the mare "WHOA." The mare is

9.18. *This mare is half-jumping the log. Her front end is jumped over, but she is stopped before she comes over with her back feet.*

9.19. *Half-jumps are usually followed by a sidepass off the obstacle.*

then held still until Barbara can settle her and "get it all together"; then the mare is sidepassed off the jump.

In teaching the half-jump from the ground, lead the horse over and give him a firm "WHOA" as his front end clears. In the beginning, you'll probably have to take hold of his shank and hold him in place so he doesn't jump over with his back feet. Stop him and stand him several moments, praising him with a pat or by voice for getting the idea. Then, either sidepass him over by steadying his head and pushing him over with your hand against his sides, or lead him off the jump. Again, this is something you don't do too often, once you have given the horse the idea of what it's all about. Too much half-jumping, as with too much stopping after jumps, will inhibit your horse's hunterlike form in jumping.

From the saddle, jump the front end over, say "WHOA" with good timing, have contact with the head—but don't JERK on the horse. Hold him there and settle him, then sidepass or step him off. When practicing the sidepass off, take him off a different way each time, so he doesn't anticipate your cue.

WHAT CAN YOU EXPECT IN THE SHOW RING?

Jumps are usually simple in size and basic type, but are often made somewhat spooky by having tarps, hides, or brush set across them. You can watch trail classes before you actually begin showing in them to get an idea of how the jumps will be varied. When you see something a little different, try to set the same thing up at home to school on. To be ready for the show ring variations, teach your horse to jump regular jumps, ones with tarps, hides, even children's furry jackets laid over the pole. Cut brush to drape over your obstacle. Jump bales of hay, small benches, fallen logs out on the trail—anything "different" you can think of. Of course, you'll often just have a simple pole jump in the show ring, but very often, someone with a vivid imagination will make the jump a little spooky.

Chapter Ten

Bridges

Originally, a bridge on a trail course was just the type of obstacle you would ride over if you were crossing water or some sort of ditch while riding out on the trail. It was simple. You just rode up, gave the horse his head so he could investigate, then you crossed. Nowadays, however, bridges are becoming more like trick platforms than functional "cross-overs." If you don't instill confidence in your horse from his first experience on a bridge, he'll never accept the difficult bridge obstacles seen in many show rings today.

The best way to start a horse on working bridges is to lay either a heavy, flat sheet of plywood on the ground, or a platform consisting of something about the size of 2×4s, not more than two inches off the ground. It should be wide enough that the horse doesn't have a rough time staying on it.

Begin with leading the horse onto the bridge. If he's scared, don't stop him! Keep him going right across it. Take him over three or four times, even if he's rushing. After going over this many times, he'll begin to understand that it's no big deal. Then, you can take him on, stop him, pet him, and teach him to relax on the bridge.

When he's working well on the low platform, you can start leading him over different types of bridges, teaching him to relax on any bridge you take him on. He should, whenever possible, be led over a raised railed bridge, preferably both the step-up and ramp type. When you have his confidence, you can begin riding him over.

In the beginning, when you know he's been over the bridges during the leading sessions, you are aware that he shouldn't refuse the bridge. If he does, use your legs to keep driving him forward and work to put him onto the center of the bridge. If he comes on a little crooked, particularly on a railed bridge, you might hit a stirrup on the rail, or even hang one up on a rail board. This could panic a nervous horse and hurt you. If you find your horse wanting to rush somewhat, stop him right before he goes on the bridge and make him stand. Move him up so his front feet are on the bridge and stop and stand him again. Let him go a step or two more, then hold him there. Use the "stop-start" method of taking him all the way across the bridge to be sure he does it carefully.

10.1. Leading a green horse over a bridge helps him become confident.

When your horse is taking the bridge slowly and calmly, teach him to drop his head and look at it, as he should be doing with his stepovers. Take him up to the bridge, stop him, and make him drop his head before going over. Keep cuing him to remain "looking down" until he's over the bridge and his back feet are off. When a horse drops and looks at the bridge, the judge will feel this horse is really investigating the obstacle for it's safety. Out on the trail, you wouldn't *want* a horse that would go right over anything without taking a good look at it—you might put him across a bridge too weak to hold him. This is what you want in the trail course—a show horse that has "out-on-the-trail-sense" and isn't going to go over something without taking a look at it first.

Low and railed bridges are best for beginning schooling. After the horse is further along, you can work him on a railless raised bridge such as the one in the photos on page 190. Here the palomino is going over it, stepping in the tire. Never take a horse over a bridge like this unless he is completely relaxed, and goes calmly over lower bridges. If he were to step off the side of this type of bridge and hurt himself, he'd become quite afraid of bridges in general.

Varying Bridges

Show ring trail classes often disguise bridges to make the horse take a really good look. Some are so covered with brush that they look like gardens. At home, to be prepared for just about anything, change your bridge frequently by adding different obstacles to it.

If you can cut fresh brush, small tree branches, or bushes, lay them on the floor of the bridge and string them through the rails. One show we attended had placed cut flowers on the brush which was laid on the bridge floor. The bright yellow flowers almost caused a couple of horses to refuse. So if you can, throw some flowers down on the bridge.

10.2. Bridges are often tricky in the show ring. This is a teetering bridge with a precarious stepover elevated right at the step-off point. You must school at home to be prepared for anything!

Rails are often placed on bridges. A single pole can be laid down so that the horse steps up on the bridge, has to step over the pole, then off the bridge. This is relatively simple to school a horse for. Be sure he is looking closely and doesn't get lazy and hit the pole. Ride him up to the bridge, stop and drop his head (when you're schooling at home). Let him step up on the bridge, stop him and drop his head down so he can take a close look at the pole. Then, step him over and off the bridge. Next time, take him straight across with his head dropped. He should have no trouble with a single pole. If you feel he's ready for more difficulty, place two parallel rails on the bridge, just far enough apart for him to take a short step.

Poles are often set up in trail courses before and after a bridge so that the horse must step over them as he comes up to and leaves the bridge. If you look at the photo taken at Cow Palace on page 186, of the rider coming off the ramp-type bridge, you can see how closely the elevated pole was located, and how "flimsy" the bases used for elevation are. If a horse touched it only slightly, it would fall. This, by the way, is a teetering bridge and a horse has a tendency to slide into the pole unless worked extremely carefully. How would you school for such "trick obstacles"?

Start at home by setting a stepover two strides ahead of the bridge. Ride the horse up, step him over, then take him up to and over the bridge. Be sure he's relaxed and competent, then add another pole two strides off the bridge. Take him around, ride him over the first stepover, over the bridge, then over the second stepover. If he rushes a little, or doesn't pay attention, use some "stop-start" schooling. Ride him up to the first pole, stop him and drop his head. Make him stand there quietly. After a while, cue him to move on and let him step over the pole only with his front feet, and stop him again. Then step him up to the point where his front feet are on the bridge, and stop him again. Remember that many horses, after going on a bridge, want to come off fast. This exercise is especially good at slowing them down. If they rush off a bridge with a stepover to maneuver, they'll knock it down. Just "creep him across" the bridge, and stop him when his front feet are off. Hold him awhile, walk him off the rest of the way and up to the stepover. Stop him, drop his head, then take him over. The whole purpose is to teach him to go slowly and carefully.

COURTESY OF
BROWN'S ARABIANS

10.3. *Teaching a horse to accept a tire on a bridge takes patience.*
At this point, The Horseradish Kid would like to take me for a ride—
anywhere but across the bridge!

Though you wouldn't stop him before, during, or while coming off the bridge in the show ring, you have to use this schooling at home so he WILL go slowly in a show.

Increase the difficulty by moving the poles closer into the bridge. Move them in at first so the horse has one good stride between the poles and the bridge. Later, you can squeeze them in a little more. If the horse seems a little clumsy, use something heavier as a substitute for the poles. Railroad ties work fine. The horse knows they're substantial and if he touches them with his feet, he'll start picking them up higher!

TIRE-AND-BRIDGE COMBINATIONS

There are horses who are well schooled on working tires and well schooled on plain bridges, but somehow, when you put the two together, the horse isn't quite sure exactly what he's supposed to do. Look at the picture of The Horseradish Kid on page 188 who seems to think the tire on the bridge is getting ready to bite him. He's trying his best to duck off. To cure his jitters, he was ridden up until his front feet were on the bridge and asked to stand quietly until he had relaxed and taken a long look at the tire. He was then moved up until a front foot was placed in the tire and held still. After this, he was slowly moved off the bridge. The "stop-start" method worked after one time. He hasn't balked at a bridge-tire combination since.

Just be sure that you never try a tire on a bridge unless your horse is competent at working tires away from the bridge, as was Horseradish. Never introduce a new obstacle, such as showing a horse tires for the first time, by placing them on another obstacle. A horse needs confidence. He gets that by learning one thing at a time, THEN having them combined.

When a horse is calmly working a railed bridge with a tire, and isn't likely to try to evade stepping in the tire center, you can begin schooling for railless bridges and tires. The palomino gelding in the photos on page 190 is being worked on just that—

10.4. Mock Won negotiates a tire on a railless bridge with ease and confidence.

10.5. Notice how calmly and carefully he begins to step off.

a fairly high railless bridge with a tire in the center. He is negotiating it beautifully and comes off the bridge slowly and carefully. This is a beginning for an even more difficult obstacle.

Wendy Daniels, riding Candy Bar, was asked to work a railless bridge with three tires at the Junior Grand National at the Cow Palace. You can see (photo below) that the tires weren't especially small. When the horse walked up and placed a foot in the tire, the other foot had to reach over the tire and onto the bridge. The next step brought a foot out of the first tire,

10.6. Wendy Daniels takes Candy Bar across a bridge and tire combination at the Junior Grand National. They went clean on this obstacle.

10.7. *In another bridge-tire combination, Wendy and Candy have to leave the bridge, walk a stride, and step into a tractor tire and begin a pivot.*

trying to reach for the second. In the case of a small mare, like Candy, this took a lot of coordination and "reaching." Candy's home-schooling accounts for her success. You should also school at home.

Start the three-tire combination by only using *two* tires. Set the first one two strides before the bridge, and second two strides away. Work them in the same manner as the stepover poles, moving them in gradually. When the horse is doing a perfect jog and is relaxed and happy with working the two tires before and after the bridge, place the third tire on the bridge and work with all three.

TEETERING BRIDGES

Shows are using teetering bridges quite a bit, and some horses aren't prepared for it, because they haven't been properly schooled at home. It's not natural for a horse to walk up on something that's going to tip and move! This is another point in training where confidence plays a great role.

In the photo of Dusty on page 193, Barbara is leading him up on a small ramp bridge with a tire set under one end to elevate it. Because Dusty is coming along so quickly in his schooling, he'll stay on this type of narrow bridge. In starting *your* horse on teetering bridges, I would suggest you use a railed bridge and place a tire under its end. As the horse is led up and across, the end of the bridge sinks just a little, introducing the horse to feeling movement in the bridge. Work him on it until he is totally relaxed.

The next step would be to place a 2×4 under the bridge *center* placed so that the bridge is elevated by the two-inch side. This keeps the movement from being too drastic at first. The diagram on page 196 shows you how to place the board under the bridge. Lead the horse up and stand him with his

10.8. *A good introduction to the feel of a teetering bridge is a platform or bridge with a tire placed under the end so it gives and moves the bridge a little as the horse steps.*

10.9, 10.10, 10.11. In this obstacle, the horse is required to step up on the bridge, do a turn on the forehand with his front feet up, sidepass the length of the bridge, do another turn on the forehand, go up all the way on the bridge, and ride across.

front feet on the bridge, stop, and pet him. Move him up just a bit until the bridge starts to rock a little. Then hold and pet him to get him to relax. Many horses want to run off a teetering bridge—be careful to stay out of your horse's way in case he tries. The original concept on working bridges was to keep the horse going over three or four times and not stop him when he was scared. Since he's had all the basics before starting teetering bridge work, you won't have to worry so much about keeping him going, but more on slowing him down. Use the "stop-start" method a lot to get him to work it slowly.

Eventually, you should be able to place a 4×4 under the bridge to make it teeter more. Your horse should accept it if

10.12, 10.13. After riding over the bridge, the horse is allowed to come off only with his front feet. He then does a turn on the haunches to go around the corner, sidepass the entire bridge, does another turn on the haunches, then is ridden off.

10.A. Setting up a teetering bridge (viewed from above).

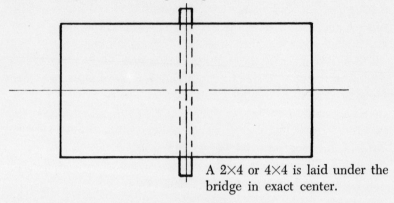

A 2×4 or 4×4 is laid under the bridge in exact center.

he was brought along slowly enough in the basic schooling. From here, get him to work a teetering railless bridge, and begin riding him over the bridges, starting with the basics and getting to the bridge with the 4×4.

ARE BRIDGES BECOMING TRICK PLATFORMS?

Yes! Many trail classes are asking for bridges in combination with other obstacles. I've often seen an L-shaped backthrough set on the side of the bridge. The horse must be ridden up to the bridge center and backed off the side right into the backthrough obstacle. You must school your horse at home to turn on a bridge, back off a railless bridge, or step off the side of it.

An even more hair-raising obstacle is becoming popular in some of the bigger shows. In the photos of Barbara and Frosty on page 194, you can see the pair practicing at home. When they were first asked to work this at a show, the bridge was the type that raised up and peaked in the middle, making it even more difficult than this flat bridge.

In the first photo, Frosty is ridden up so only his front feet are on the bridge. Next, Barbara asks him for a turn on the forehand to bring him around to the bridge side where he must sidepass the length of the bridge. On the other end, still another turn on the forehand, then he must go up on the bridge with his back feet and walk across it.

The next photos show the other way they have been asked to work a bridge in the show ring. Frosty was ridden up on the bridge and across it, only being allowed to leave the bridge with his front feet. He is settled, then does a turn on the haunches to get into position to sidepass the length of the bridge. After doing another turn on the haunches at the other end, he was ridden off.

Before you ever try to school on such a difficult obstacle, be sure that your horse is competent at working any type of bridge, and is *thoroughly* schooled on his turns on the forehand, on the haunches, and his sidepassing. Work it SLOWLY at home, taking only one small step at a time. This requires so much confidence in a horse that you must be terribly careful not to hurt him. Take it easy!

BE READY FOR ANYTHING!

School at home so you can produce a horse who accepts any bridge, whether it be laden with tarps, hides, tires, poles or brush. Confidence is the name of the game. Work at producing it!

Chapter Eleven

All Those "Strange" Things!

Course designers can get quite imaginative when adding "different" types of obstacles, separate from the usual gates, bridges, stepovers, and backthroughs. Sometimes, they get a little carried away, like the time at a large Southern California show when an elephant was tethered on the trail course and exhibitors were asked to ride past it. Since trail classes are *supposed* to simulate conditions you might run across while out riding on the trail, I sincerely hope I never ride ANY horse so far that I wind up in elephant country!

You do have to be ready to face some strange things in trail classes. The courses just have to be tougher these days. In the past, when courses were made up of simple gates, bridges, stepovers, and backthroughs, nearly every horse in the class would go clean, and the tie breaker would be the rail work. That makes it more of a pleasure than a trail class. For this reason, you'll find courses becoming more difficult and "different." Your horse will face everything from plastic tarps and hides, to ducks, geese, chickens, and pigs, and he'll have to face them with evident calmness. He may have to be roped from, or just drag something with a rope. There are a multitude of "strange" things they're asking trail horses to do and the way to get ready for them is to school at home to produce a horse that is so confident and so well broke, he will accept just about anything. Let's look at some of the things you can do in your home-schooling.

GET HIM USED TO A ROPE!

Many trail classes ask for contestants to drag an object at the end of a rope. Sometimes, you ride forward and pull it behind you; at other times, you back and drag it out where the horse *has* to watch it move "toward him." This spooks a lot of horses more than dragging it behind them, especially if it's something noisy, like a sack full of tin cans. In some shows, you'll see horses going absolutely crazy over a rope/drag situation and if a rider has dallied too tight or taken more than one wrap, he often can't get the rope loose enough to get rid of it before he gets into trouble. To keep this from happening, you need to do two things. First, get your horse used to the rope and the concept of dragging an object. Second, learn to dally correctly.

If you've ever seen a roper schooling a green horse, you know how quietly and easily they go about getting a horse accustomed to a rope. The rider will lay the rope on the horse's neck, drape it down on the hindquarters and bring it along the side. He'll be sure to let the rope hang and let it touch the horse on the lower part of his legs. The horse has to learn to accept the rope touching him anywhere on his body. In the case of a trail horse, it's particularly important that he learns to accept having the rope lay across his hocks, in case he ever has to make a turn while dragging an obstacle. If the rider rides off to the left (the rope is on the right), the rope is naturally going to go around the hocks.

In the photos (see p. 200), you can see how Wendy uses her rope to get Candy Bar used to having it anywhere on her body. In addition to doing this, you can rig your horse up as though you were going to ground-drive him—with two lines—one on

11.1. *Wendy schools at home, getting Candy Bar used to a rope.*

11.2, 11.3. *A trail horse should accept having the rope touch any part of the body from front . . . to back.*

each side, running from the bit, through the stirrups, and back behind him. Drive your horse and step off to the side when you turn him. When you ask for a left turn, step off to the left and direct rein him with the left rein. At the same time, lay the right line over his hocks so it's rubbing on him while he moves. You don't want to *tighten* the rope or it'll pull your horse in the opposite direction of the turn. Just lay it over his hocks and get him used to it. You can also longe your horse by not running the line closest to you through the stirrup, but directly from a *halter* (not a bit) to your hands. The other line would go from the halter, through the off-side stirrup, and directly around the horse's hindquarters, over his hocks, to your hands. All the time you're longeing him, the rope is working across his hocks, and he gets used to it.

When your horse doesn't seem to mind the presence of a rope, put some sand or dirt in a gunny sack and use it for a drag obstacle. Don't make it very heavy at first—just fill it one-

11.4. Wendy often ropes her "hay-bale steer" when schooling her mare.

third or one-fourth full of sand or dirt and tie it shut. Attach your rope so it won't slip off. At this stage, you'll either want someone to hand you your end of the rope, or you'll want to lay it up on a fence or on something that you can ride up to. Don't try mounting and dismounting with the rope the first time you have something on the end of it. Play it safe.

When you pick up your end of the rope, try to position yourself so the sack is in the center of an imaginary circle and you can then ride around and around the sack. The horse will feel the tension on the rope, but the sack won't actually be dragging enough to worry him at first. This is the way a lot of ropers start "logging" their horses. The horse moves around in a circle, just moving, but not dragging the log. You should do this with your trail horse with his sack. When he's quiet and doesn't seem to mind the tension on the rope, straighten him out a little so he's pulling the sack off at an angle. When you feel you can do it successfully, ride straight off, dragging the sack behind you. The rope is going to lie across the side of the horse's hip, and he might jump a little, so you might prefer not to have the rope dallied while you do this. Just hold it in your hand.

You may have to spend several sessions working slowly on this. Take as much time as you need. Some horses accept a rope readily, others are afraid. When your horse is pulling a rope well, make him turn, face it, and back while pulling the sack. When he's doing well with the sack, try dragging a small log, a sack of cans, a hide or simulated hide (old furry jackets are good)—anything "strange" you can think of.

How to Dally

When you dally to drag something, you should do so carefully, not only to assure that you can do a quick release, but also to protect your fingers from getting caught in between the rope and the horn. There is an old term called "roper's

11.5. Candy accepts dragging a sack of cans.

thumb," and if you want to see what it is, check the rope hand of a few old ropers. You're bound to find a man who's lost a thumb in a dally during team roping. Although you'll only be dallying with a sack or log at the end—not a big steer— you *can* still get hurt if you don't pay attention to what you're doing.

Check the pictures of Wendy on page 204. The rope is on the right side of her horse when she takes it. She dallies by taking one counterclockwise wrap around the horn, keeping

11.6. Facing the sack of cans and backing while dragging it along.

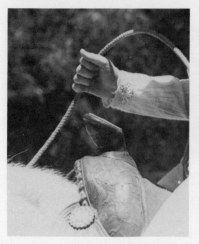
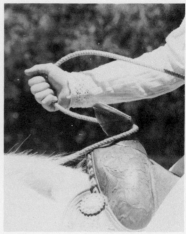

11.7. When you begin your dally, maintain enough slack so you don't get your fingers hung up between the horn and the rope.

11.8. Wrap in a counterclockwise direction.

11.9. This is a one-wrap dally, generally sufficient for the lightweight objects you'll be asked to drag in the show ring. You can keep your rope hand in this position.

11.10. Setting your rope hand down on your leg is another position you can use for a one-wrap dally.

her hand far enough away from the horn that she doesn't get her fingers caught. After the dally, she can either hold the rope up higher than the horn, or bring it down on her leg. Seldom, in a trail class, will you dally up on something so big and heavy that you have to take more than one dally, or can't hold it by having your hand down on your leg. Remember that one dally comes off FAST if your horse gets too excited to hold on to the rope. Two dallies are unnecessary, and you lose time, if you have to get undone quickly.

That Noisy Sack of Cans

Sacks full of tin cans are often used in trail classes. Generally, you'll have to pick up the sack off a barrel or post, ride to the designated point, and drop the sack off or hang it on another post. Once, at the Cow Palace, a sack of cans was tied to the end of a rope and were placed on the seat of a covered wagon. Riders had to dally up to the rope and ride off, dragging the obstacle until the sack of cans fell off the wagon and hit the ground. You can imagine the reaction of some horses when the cans crashed to the ground behind them. Get your horse used to accepting the cans. Some horses just never accept them fully, but you have to work to get as much acceptance from them as possible.

Put *some* cans in a gunny sack. Avoid making it big and bulky. At home we school with a sack roughly containing twenty empty cat-food and soft-drink cans. It's light, easy to carry, yet still noisy enough to serve the purpose. When we first introduce a horse to the cans, we do it in an enclosed area, such as a corral or round pen, and put a halter and long rope on him. We stand away from him and gently wiggle the cans. It won't do any good to just walk right at a horse shaking cans in his face! Get him used to it while you're standing ten feet or so away. Spend several sessions standing off from him, if he really acts afraid of the cans, and just gradually get closer each. time. Some horses will let you walk right up with the cans the first day, others will seem terrified. Give him as much time as he needs to get used to the cans and when he'll let you, run the sack along his sides and up on his back.

If you get a horse used to the cans from the ground first, he should readily accept it when you try riding him with the cans. Pick the sack up off a barrel or fence and ride around with them *without* shaking them at first. If he jumps a little off to the side the first time you ride and pick them up, try to relax him without causing a big scene. Let him calm down and stand until he accepts the cans, then ride off.

Gradually get the horse used to having you shake the cans. Make quite a bit of noise. If you have to ride up in a class and take the cans in your hand and ride to another spot, you'll score more points by shaking those cans hard and prove your

11.11. Wendy dismounts to pick up and carry a sack of tin cans.

11.12. She keeps contact with Candy while picking up the cans.

horse accepts them, then by picking them up and carrying them as if you're afraid he'll hear them. You should be able to pick the sack up and move your hand up and down quickly —that really starts those cans moving!

MOUNTING AND DISMOUNTING WITH AN OBSTACLE

You never know when you're going to be asked to dismount, pick up an obstacle and mount the horse with it. It might be a sack of cans, or a bucket of water, or even in some cases, a live animal! I once saw photos of an Arabian show trail class

11.13. Gathering her reins and a handful of mane in her left hand, she holds the cans up.

11.14. Here she lays the cans over the saddle while she mounts.

11.15. After mounting, she shakes the cans. A rider who "makes some noise" with those cans will score more than the one who doesn't.

11.16. *In a show ring situation, Kari Haas picks up a sack of cans from a post.*

11.17. *She shakes them noisily while she rides Shaugnessey Dee across a bridge. Kari won this class.*

where riders had to mount while holding a huge, live goose by the feet. A show might have you carry something like a baby goat from one point to another.

The most important thing to remember is to keep constant control on your horse when you mount and dismount with something in your hand. Gather your reins up with one hand and keep contact. In the case of a sack of cans, as shown in the photos of Wendy mounting on page 207, you can lay it over the seat of the saddle until you can get up. However, when using a bucket of water, hold it out away from the horse so it doesn't tip and spill. Practice at home until you find the way that is easiest for YOU.

MOUNTING ON THE "WRONG" SIDE

In a trail class I recently competed in, we were asked to dismount on the left side, lead the horse over a jump, then mount on the right side. If you practice this at home, most horses will accept it. The important thing is to be sure the horse is made to stand completely still. This is awkward for a rider when he's been left-side mounting all his life! If your horse is still and cooperative, you can look a lot better in your attempts to mount on the right side. Practice it at home as often as possible, so you can do it gracefully.

Water Obstacles

Whenever possible, ride your horse out into natural water obstacles, such as creeks, streams, or just large "mud puddles."

11.18. Whenever possible, getting a horse used to natural water will help in schooling on man-made water obstacles.

11.19. Wendy's father made her this water box by building a wooden frame and lining it with a plastic tarp.

11.20. The box is varied by adding brush around the edge and a pole across the center.

If a horse accepts natural water, he's more likely to accept such things as artificial water obstacles, from boxes to pools. If a horse is reluctant to enter water, it often helps to school him on a very large, but not too deep, body of water. Have one well-schooled horse go in ahead of him and another right behind him. It will box him in and also give him some confidence, because the other horses are well schooled in entering the water and do it without fear.

When we take a reluctant horse in the water for the first time, we find it an advantage to do it after a long ride when the horse is tired and thirsty and NOT when he's fresh out of the stall. If a horse refuses to go in with a horse in front and behind him, it often helps to use a reliable pony horse

11.21. A small plastic dish-pan, with a running hose, makes a good schooling obstacle for Good News.

to dally the halter rope to and literally "drag" the horse in. If the horse sets back a lot, keep the pony horse moving in a circle around him to unlock him, then move straight out. Once a horse is in the water for the first time, the problem is nearly over. If he takes a nice long drink and you make him stand there and relax a while, he'll learn to like it.

When a horse works well and goes right into water out on the trail, he'll be likely to accept a water box. If you want to make a water hole on your trail course, dig a wide hole, not more than a foot deep, and place a plastic tarp in it to keep the water from seeping down into the dirt and the hole from drying up. If the horse is spooky about the tarp, cover it with some dirt before you fill the hole.

Water boxes, such as the one shown in the photo of Wendy and Candy on page 210, can be made with straight wood construction, and a plastic tarp placed inside and over the edges to hold the water. You can vary this, as Wendy has, by adding brush, poles, or tires.

Some shows make water boxes extremely spooky by adding dry ice to them. It would be a good idea to school on this at home, as well as pouring some laundry detergent into the water and turning the hose on full force to make a huge pile of bubbles. Anything you can do to pair up your water obstacle with another obstacle is also good for schooling. Place the water box right next to the edge of a bridge, so the horse has to walk off the bridge right into the water. Use your imagination!

Farm Animals

Many courses cage up such things as chickens, ducks, or geese, or put animals on a rope and tether them on the course. I've seen courses where a rider had to mount while holding a sack full of chickens. A trail horse has to accept just about anything including other animals!

At one local show a few years ago, there was a pig tethered near the bridge, and the horses had to ride by it. The problem this brought about was that the first few horses startled the pig—it ran and hit the end of its rope. Later, it became used to the horses and just lay down. This makes it a little unfair in some respects if you have no choice about the order in which you enter the class. If I *had* the choice in a situation like this, I would go in early if I had a horse who accepted such an animal moving quickly. It would look good to the judge if the horse didn't spook "wildly" over the pig. If I had a horse that was terrified of pigs, I'd try to get in toward the end of the class, when the pig had settled down.

Pigs are a big cause of "nerves" in many horses. After all, they don't smell so good, and they move quickly and often make a lot of noise. If you have the chance to get your trail horse into a situation where he MUST accept this sort of ani-

11.22. Barnyard-type animals are often tethered to a section of a show ring trail course. Both my trail horse and I agreed that this was the STRANGEST looking goat we'd ever seen!

mal, take advantage of it. We turned one of our "pig haters" into a pasture where two pigs shared an adjoining corral. The other pasture horses were used to the pigs and stood near them all day. Our horse wouldn't go near that end of the pasture for the first two days, but after that, we found him standing near the pigs with the other horses, and to this day, he doesn't care who the pig belongs to or where it is! He'll walk right past it or stop and look at it—whatever you ask him to do.

One trainer I know who had a couple of horses that were afraid of geese, bought two adult geese and gave them the run of the stable for a few weeks. It cured the horses of their fear and they began to accept the geese as just another part of the stable. We have a small goat that has the run of the stable area and sometimes climbs right in the troughs to eat with our horses. As a result, they accept goats with ease, and you'll *often* find a goat on a trail course.

Those of you who live on cattle ranches or have the opportunity to help out with the moving or branding of cattle have a good thing going for your trail horses! At one large show, the gate obstacle was worked so that the horses were taken

11.23. Mr. Golddust follows "Honker," a goose which has the free run of this training stable. The trail horses here accept him readily and should accept this type of animal in the show ring.

11.24. Candy Bar has "her own" goat, Annabelle.

through the gate right into a pen full of calves. They had to move the calves around the pen, and go out another gate. Needless to say, startled calves can move quickly, and many "city-raised" horses have never seen a cow. Anytime you have the chance to be around cattle with your trail horses, take advantage of it.

Just to let you know how "hairy" a trail course can be, the final obstacle in the Cow Palace's first Grand Prix trail class was to ride into and close a bucking chute. The rodeo, held each year with the Cow Palace show, provided not only the use of the chutes, but also the use of two large bulls—one for the chute in front of the trail horse, and one behind.

BE READY FOR ANYTHING

Whenever you see an obstacle at a show, try to find a way to practice it at home. Set up a mailbox so you can ride up to it and pull out a tarp or slicker, or even a small animal, such as a rabbit. Pony another horse off yours. Teach your horse to accept being ridden double. Picking up and carrying an additional rider is often a part of trail classes. Get your horse used to hides and furs. Having a deerhunter in the family can be an asset. Hides can be used to rope and drag, or draped on a gate or bridge. Wendy used a leopard coat and teddy bear to make a "strange creature" to put on her bridge while schooling Candy. Use your imagination to come up with the most "wild and woolly" obstacles you can think of to school on at home. Then, when you come to a show and see something that has all the riders sitting around saying "What the heck is THAT?!", you'll know you can work it successfully with your horse.

11.25. Some shows require the rider carry an animal during a trail course. Wendy practices with her dog, Thorton.

Chapter Twelve

Sidepass Obstacles

The biggest favor you can do for your trail horse to help him properly work sidepass obstacles is to be SURE you teach him *away* from the trail course before ever asking him to sidepass on an obstacle. And, while you're at it, he'd better know how to back easily, and do a turn on the forehand and haunches. Why? Because many obstacles require a combination of these, even though they are considered "sidepass obstacles."

When a horse properly sidepasses an obstacle, he does it slowly, carefully, showing a good attitude. If a horse is soured on sidepassing, he'll become the kind of horse you have to *make* do things by using harder and harder leg pressure, going to spurs and eventually, using just plain force. Attitude is SO important in a trail horse, and you have to work especially hard to instill a good attitude and frame of mind on sidepass obstacles. You're aiming to produce a horse who *relaxes* when working a sidepass.

The way to get a horse to relax and accept a sidepass obstacle is to start with very simple moves. Work extremely slowly and gradually build up the difficulty *without* building up speed. Change your obstacles frequently so the horse isn't sidepassing "that same old log" out of sheer habit. A horse that habitually works the same obstacle tries to rush to finish.

12.1. Wendy uses heavy poles, elevated on small standards, for schooling on a straight sidepass.

He'll begin sidepassing on his own before you even have him set up properly, and he'll "fly" through the obstacle.

So, let's start a gradual difficulty build-up and begin by working a very simple sidepass. Take a heavy pole, such as a jump pole, and lay it on the ground. Keep it away from other obstacles so all the horse has to worry about is that one object. In the beginning, the horse has to get the concept of having his front feet on one side of the pole and his back feet on the other, so ride slowly up to the center of the pole. Stop your horse and let him look at the pole, as you would if schooling him on a stepover. Gather him up and leg him forward lightly until his front feet are over the pole and *gently* ask him to stop. Don't jerk on his head and scream "WHOA!," or you're off to a bad start! Just gather him up, say "whoa" quietly and hold him there. Stand and relax him for a few minutes.

When you're ready to sidepass to the left, gather him up and use light hand and leg aids to sidepass him one or two steps, then STOP. You're trying to teach him to *creep*, not rush, to the side. After a step or two, quietly tell him "whoa" and release your leg aids. Hold him there awhile, then ask for another step or two. Keep this up until you've sidepassed completely off the obstacle, and hold him there a few moments. If a horse isn't taken completely off the obstacle before being ridden away from it, he'll begin "leaving" when he feels like it. You have to hold him there and make him wait for YOU to make the decision of whether you'll ride straight away from it, back away, or just stand there for a long time. Keep him guessing and he won't start anticipating.

School your horse to step over the log and sidepass off in either direction with equal ease. Take time during several sessions to work this type of obstacle, but be sure to change the location of the pole. If he's only sidepassed on that pole at one spot, he might not grasp the concept of ever sidepass-

ing at any other location. Many horses blow up in the show
ring because they're not taught to obediently work an obstacle anyplace, anytime.

SPACING

Throughout this early schooling and on into the "rough
stuff," pay careful attention to properly positioning your horse
for the sidepass. Many people misjudge the "center" of a horse,
and he MUST be properly centered in relation to the pole
or other obstacle. If he's not, his front or back legs will hit
the obstacle. Not only does this lose points in the show ring,
but if the horse is asked to sidepass something large, such as
a heavy barrel, he's liable to hurt himself if he hits it with
his legs. If he's hurt, he loses confidence.

Where is the "center"? It's farther back than you might
think. Chances are, it's close to the point where your back
cinch rigging is. If you could draw a line straight down from
there, possibly just in front of it, the concept of centering the
obstacle under your horse would become clearer. What you're
trying for is an equal distance between the front of the obstacle and the horse's front legs, and the back of the obstacle
and the horse's back legs. If you're going to sidepass a jump
pole, you have plenty of room to play with. If you're using
a big telephone pole or barrel, then you'll have less distance
between the obstacle and the legs, which makes it a little
tougher to get correctly spaced. If you ride as we do on the
West Coast, with your legs hanging well under you, you could
draw a straight line down through the shoulder, hip, and on
to the heel. Your heel is then going to be right about at that
center point, just in front of where the back cinch would be.
If you're sidepassing a big obstacle, like a telephone pole or
barrel, you can center your horse by positioning so that your
heel is centered on the width of the obstacle.

On to More Schooling

When you're a "pro" at getting centered and have worked your horse at sidepassing by first stepping him over the pole, you should have no trouble in beginning to line up for the sidepass in the same way you would at a show. Rather than stepping over a pole, ride straight up so the end of the pole is visible to you and you can get centered easily. If you begin too far from the pole, you're liable to cause your horse to lose the concept of sidepassing the obstacle. Get up even closer with a green horse. Stop and make him stand after you're centered, then start your "one-step-at-a-time" schooling and move him all the way for the sidepass, stopping him when he's cleared it. Be sure to practice it in both directions.

Once you're sure your horse is confident in his sidepassing, you can go from straight simple obstacles to slightly more difficult ones. In the photos on page 222, you can see Wendy sidepassing Candy on the L-shaped obstacle. In the first photo, she is at the point where the horse's back end must be held and the front end taken around the turn. It's a simple turn on the haunches. In the second shot, she is straight, well spaced, and is moving off, sidepassing to the left. In the third photo, she has cleared the obstacle. Before working on this obstacle, Candy was schooled on straight sidepassing on the straight raised-pole backthrough. She sidepassed with her front feet "in" the obstacle in both instances.

A good obstacle for schooling, which is often used in the show ring, is the "M"-shaped pole obstacle, that Wendy is working in the photo on page 224. The diagram on page 223 explains how it is to be worked step by step. As with all sidepass obstacles, the important thing here is to get your proper spacing in the beginning and *keep* it throughout.

Look at position "A" on the diagram. The horse has been

12.3. *Candy is working a sidepass L. She is going to the left and has reached the corner. Her back end is held still and her front end has moved around the corner—a turn on the haunches.*

12.4. *The body is straight again, and they're sidepassing the second section. Notice how Wendy maintains a fairly normal body position in the saddle, and can look to see her position by moving only her head—not by leaning way over the side, a move which would throw the mare off balance.*

12.5. *The mare is moved clear off the end of the sidepass before being allowed to move away, or walk straight away from it.*

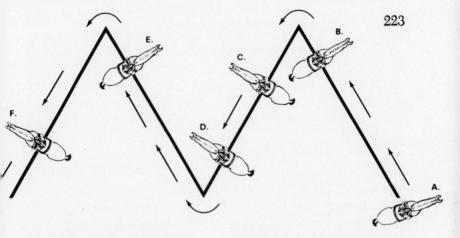

12.A. Sidepassing the "M" poles.

A. Position your horse so the pole is exactly in the center of his front and back legs. Sidepass him to point "B."

B. At this point, begin a turn on the haunches, with the back end staying in place and the front end *clearing the point*, pivoting, and putting the horse into point "C."

C. Sidepass to the next point.

D. Hold the front end here and do a turn on the forehand—the front stays in place and the back legs pivot around the corner.

E. After sidepassing to this point, hold the back end steady and pivot the front end around the point—another turn on the haunches.

F. Sidepass off the pole.

ridden into position with the pole spaced correctly in the center between his front and back legs. He is then carefully sidepassed to point "B." This is where spacing is especially crucial. Remember, you're trying to work this obstacle without the horse touching the poles. At point "B," you're ready to begin a turn on the haunches, that is, you hold the back end in place until you move the front end around the corner. If you start this move with the back feet too far off center— too far away from the pole—the front feet will hit the corner as they come around. So, hold your spacing, and do the turn on the forehand to get to point "C." At this point, you should be straight and well spaced to sidepass to "D," where you again must be sure that you can make the turn without hitting the poles. At this point, you do a turn on the *forehand*. The front end is held in place, and the horse is pivoted around, as his back end clears the corner. He is then straightened out and sidepassed to point "E" where he does another turn on the *haunches*. From here, he can sidepass off. If you do this obstacle SLOWLY AND CAREFULLY, with a horse that is completely schooled on the turns on the forehand and haunches as well as on sidepassing, you should be able to do it letter perfect the first time you try.

12.6. *The "M"-shaped sidepass is often seen in the show ring.*

Another tricky sidepass that is often asked for in the show ring is diagramed below. This sidepass is combined with the L-shaped backthrough. In this particular obstacle, the judge will tell you whether you're to complete the backthrough and sidepass with the back or front feet in, and also which direction the horse is to face and which way he's to sidepass. This diagram shows a sidepass with the front legs in, sidepassing to the right. "A" shows the point of entry. You work the backthrough normally until you get to point "B." Notice that the front feet are still in the obstacle, but the back feet are out. The horse is right in the center of the two poles, as he should be. To get you to point "C" all you need is a turn on the forehand. You should come out of the turn in an evenly spaced straight manner to sidepass to "D." At this point, you again hold the front end steady and bring the back end around, accomplishing another turn on the forehand. If your horse's front legs are too far forward when you start this turn, he'll hit the poles

12.B. Backing the L, then sidepassing to the right with front leg in the L.

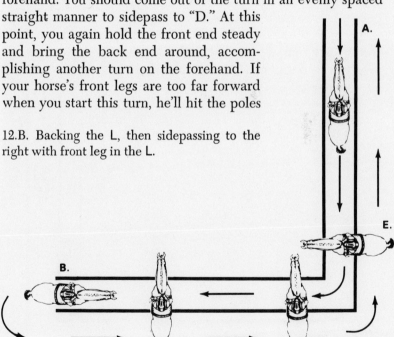

with his back feet, so be very careful about your spacing. When you get to point "E," you're home free! All you need is to sidepass off the obstacle.

How to back the L, then sidepass it to the right with the back legs "in" is shown on this page. Point "A" shows your entry. Back the L and stop at point "B." This is a little tougher. Since you want to avoid touching the poles, you should get just clear enough that the horse doesn't have to step over the poles to move his front end around, but can move just outside of them. You'd back out until his "ears" might still be in the obstacle, but his front legs would clear. You hold the back end steady, and do a turn on the haunches to point "C." Stop here to be sure you're evenly spaced, then sidepass to point "D." Remember to KEEP your spacing, or your horse is going to back into the poles. At point "D," hold the front end steady, and pivot the hind end around the corner. Be sure you're positioned to clear it. When you're at point "E," all you need do is sidepass off.

12.C. Backing the L, then sidepassing to the right with hind legs in the L.

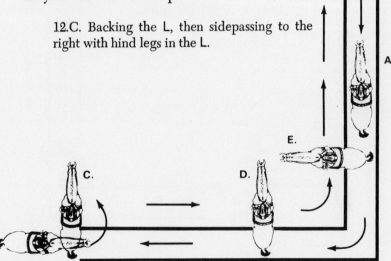

SIDEPASSING LARGER OBSTACLES

Large obstacles should never be sidepassed until the horse is VERY sure of himself in this movement. If a green horse has a tendency to step forward or back while sidepassing, work on nothing larger than a pole or log until the horse is steady.

When you do start on something larger, you can use a bale of hay set up like the one shown in the photo just below. If you're wondering about the plastic steer head on the end of the bale—Wendy likes to rope! To work this obstacle, she rode Candy up to the side and positioned her, then slowly sidepassed her to the right.

In the photo of Wendy sidepassing the barrel on page 228, you can see that when the mare (who is going to the right)

12.7. Sidepassing a bale of hay is a good practice obstacle, and one often seen in trail classes.

12.8. *Spacing is important in sidepassing an object as large as a barrel. Candy is coming in a little too close with her left front leg. Where is the "center"? In the area where the back cinch rigging would be. If Wendy's leg was more under her, she could figure the center by positioning her heel right over the center of the width of the barrel.*

moved her left front foot, she came in a little too close to the barrel. Her right front leg will come down well spaced, and her left leg will then follow or cross it, and she should be correct. If your horse is sidepassing a single barrel, you might want to try a row of two or three set end to end to make a longer, more difficult sidepass obstacle.

"Unusual" Sidepasses

One of the more difficult show obstacles is the sidepassing of a bridge while the horse has either both front feet, or both hind feet on the bridge, with the others on the ground. If you were to sidepass with the front feet on, you would probably be given instructions to ride up normally to the bridge and step the front feet up, then stop. You would then do a turn on the forehand to swing the hindquarters around the corner, and would sidepass to the other end of the bridge. Rather than sidepassing off the side, you'll usually be asked to do another turn on the forehand which puts you in position to ride up on the bridge and just ride across it.

A sidepass with the hind legs on the bridge is another tough obstacle where timing and spacing must be used to the fullest extent! You will more than likely be asked to ride across the bridge as normal, then step off with the front feet and stop while the hind legs are still on. You then do a turn on the haunches—the hind legs stay still on the bridge and the front end pivots around to put you in a position to sidepass. When you reach the other end, you'll no doubt be asked to do another pivot around the corner, then step off. (See the photos in Chap. 10.) Remember to always work this type of obstacle slowly and carefully. Don't be afraid to stop to get your bearings!

Half-jumps are often asked for in the show ring. If you check the photos in Chapter 9, you'll see Barbara on Good News, performing a half-jump. After it's completed, the horse must be positioned properly, then sidepassed off to the direction given by the judge. Chances are, your horse will complete his half-jump with his front legs a little too far ahead of the pole to begin sidepassing immediately. You'll no doubt have to gently move him back a step. In any case, you shouldn't try to begin the sidepass the instant you land when completing the jump! Give your horse a few seconds to stand there and settle, then gather him up, position him, and be sure he understands the cues to sidepass off. If you don't do it carefully, he may try to just jump the rest of the way off the pole.

COMMON MISTAKES IN SIDEPASSING

Overreining is a common mistake. When sidepassing, you control the neck, shoulders and front legs with your reins and the back portion of the horse's body with your legs. You're trying to do this so the horse is kept STRAIGHT and moves just that way. If you overrein, you produce a reverse effect. For instance, if you rein too hard to the left, you'll pull the horse's head up and off to the right and his front end will follow, making him take on a crooked position.

To correctly rein in the sidepass, try to never get your hand more than two inches from the side of the horn. By studying the photos of Wendy on Candy, you can see that in all cases, her hand is either over the top of the horn, or just barely to the side. Her mare is very well broke and reacts to extremely light rein and leg pressure. Once a horse is well schooled on sidepassing, he'll be working more off leg than rein, and you'll be more or less just keeping his body straight with your rein hand.

A lot of riders move their bodies around so much that the weight-shift throws the horse off balance, making it difficult for a horse to do a fluid, correct sidepass. If you space yourself correctly *before* you begin the sidepass, you shouldn't have to lean over to look down to see where you're positioned. You can see in the photos on page 222 that Wendy can sit square in the saddle and lean off very little to the side while sidepassing her mare. Some riders lean so far in the direction they're sidepassing, they look as though they're going to fall off the horse! Try to remain square in the saddle, moving your cue leg against the horse without a big body movement that will throw the horse off balance.

Another common mistake was touched on before, and that is the tendency for some riders to let the horse walk off, away from the sidepass before the obstacle is actually completed. If a horse walks straight away, he may have cleared the obstacle during the sidepass, but will now hit it with his hind feet as he walks away from it.

Always sidepass your horse carefully and slowly, especially when schooling at home. There should be a lot of "stop-start" schooling at home, and in the case of a horse that wants to rush, the rider should spend as much as twenty minutes working the sidepass ONCE correctly with many long pauses, rather than quickly doing it several times. Remember—a trail horse is supposed to be careful and cautious!

Chapter Thirteen

Putting It All Together

You've worked hard at home to get ready for the trail class. You've asked your horse to face countless numbers of strange and formidable obstacles. He's stood his ground and proved his worth, and you're ready for your first show. Now YOU face an obstacle—"putting it all together" to sail a smooth course you've got to pay attention to every little detail.

In most cases, long before your class is to enter the ring, the course will be posted somewhere near the arena. Particularly if the course is posted at a place where you can look at it while you look out in the arena and study the course, you have a chance to mentally "walk your course" in the same way a hunter or jumper rider does his before a class. Before riding over fences, the top rider knows how many strides he's going to take in between, where and how he's going to make his turns, and at what point of the fence he wants his horse to sail over. These same considerations are essential in showing trail horses.

Study the posted course carefully. It should tell you how the gate will be opened and the sequence of obstacles that follow. Then size up each obstacle and plan how you'll work it. Each horse is capable of different things, and a small horse that can fit in a tight situation won't work the course exactly

232

13.1. These cones are a tight squeeze, whether jogging around (in and out) or backing through.

the same as a big horse. Let's look at one example of "thinking out an obstacle."

Study the photo just above of the four cones spaced closely together. Though these were worked as a backthrough in the second class of this particular show, the instructions for the first class, novice trail horses, were for horses to jog around (in and out of) the four cones. Riders had to begin with the first cone on the left of the horse. It's easy to see that the spacing was very tight, even a snake would have difficulty "winding around them" in a fairly straight line. Since the instructions called for the obstacle to be worked at a jog, a rider had to be careful not to ask a horse to work in such a tight pattern that he'd be forced to break gait and begin walking. Also, you want your horse to work all his obstacles smoothly and fluidly. Any "jerking" to make a tight turn would ruin the appearance of your work.

How do you jog through cones spaced so tightly? Look at the diagram on page 237. You would swing way out to each side, jog a circle-type movement, come back between the next cones, jog out and around on the other side, come back through again, and so on. This gives your horse plenty of room to easily work the obstacle.

Think out each obstacle. You learn by your mistakes. You may not think one out properly until after you've failed to

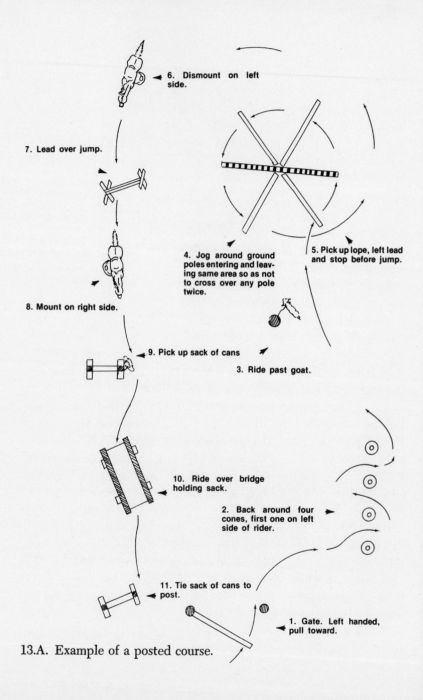

6. Dismount on left side.

7. Lead over jump.

4. Jog around ground poles entering and leaving same area so as not to cross over any pole twice.

5. Pick up lope, left lead and stop before jump.

8. Mount on right side.

9. Pick up sack of cans

3. Ride past goat.

10. Ride over bridge holding sack.

2. Back around four cones, first one on left side of rider.

11. Tie sack of cans to post.

1. Gate. Left handed, pull toward.

13.A. Example of a posted course.

work it correctly. THAT'S when you really begin using your head in advance! You soon learn, when showing trail horses, that the more thought you give to the course in advance, the less mistakes you'll make.

If you DO make a mistake on one obstacle, don't throw away the class and get careless on the rest of the course. One mistake will not entirely ruin your chances of getting in the ribbons. Maybe your horse knocked down one of the stepover poles. You're still going to score some points on that obstacle because he DID go over it and didn't refuse. He won't score as highly on that obstacle as the horse that went clean, but maybe the horse that was clean on the stepovers didn't work the gate as nicely as your horse. It all evens out.

A TYPICAL TRAIL COURSE

The series of photos beginning on page 236 were taken in an age seventeen and under trail horse class at a California show. The rider, Linda Lease, is a very successful exhibitor. Her horse is the grey Quarter Horse gelding, R.O. Major Dandy.

The photos don't begin until after the first obstacle, working the gate. The gate was worked as a left-handed, pull-toward-rider opening. When Linda closed the gate, it left her in a position to face the second obstacle. If she were NOT facing it, she would have had to plan her move before entering the ring, so she would know how to gracefully turn and go towards the next obstacle. Some riders don't think this out and look confused and lost to a judge.

The course was posted, and the judge had given instructions on the second obstacle. Horses were to be backed around the cones, with the first cone on the left of the horse. These cones were tightly spaced and Linda thought ahead of time how she would bring Dandy out far enough from each cone to turn completely around without touching the next cone. After a complete turn, she would line up and go in between

13.2. *The judge gave instructions to back around the cones, with the first cone to be on the left of the rider.*

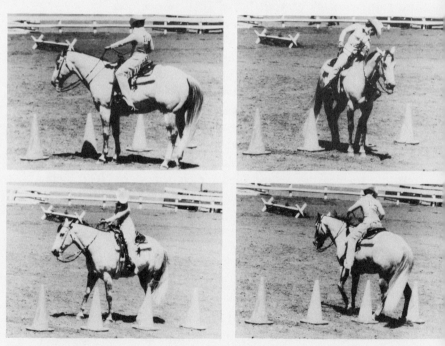

13.3, 13.4, 13.5, 13.6. *Linda Lease and R. O. Major Dandy work the obstacle well.*

13.B. "Thinking out an obstacle."

Jogging through four tightly spaced cones.

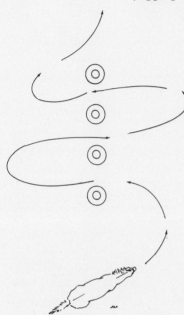

To keep the horse from breaking gait and to keep the motion fluid, riders working this obstacle had to swing way out, rather than trying to "duck in and out" staying close to the cones.

the next cones, and so on. She knew if she didn't hesitate enough to be sure of her position, she might cause Dandy to knock over a cone, which would cost points. Her careful thinking and good positioning brought Dandy through the obstacle completely clean.

The next obstacle was a "circle" of poles which riders were to jog around. There was a goat tethered about halfway between the first and second obstacle. This gave Linda a chance to let Dandy walk past the goat and have a look at it. She then picked him up at the jog as soon as she passed the goat. Why? Because PACING a horse into an obstacle is so important! Dandy needed to be at the proper jog BEFORE he got to the first pole. This would enable him to just "keep mov-

13.7. Here they're riding past a tethered goat on the way to the next obstacle.

13.8. Linda keeps Dandy moving toward the outer edge of the poles, so he can keep a more natural trotting stride and have more room to move.

ing" freely without having to change his speed—a move which might cause him to hit a pole. The instructions on this obstacle consisted of entering and exiting at the same opening, so the horse didn't jog over any of the poles twice. Linda knew that undue interference with a horse's head in a circular obstacle might cause the horse to change stride or hit a pole. By applying right leg pressure, just light enough for him to know that he was to keep moving in a circle, she arced him around. You can also see by the photos that Dandy was kept toward the outside of the circle. This allowed him more room in between each pole and more room in general to move, so he could keep a steady pace without being cramped.

The diagram of the course (see page 234) shows you at what point riders were to pick up the left lead and lope to the next point, a leadover jump. Linda knew that she'd have to stop Dandy a reasonable distance away from the jump to dismount and properly prepare him for it. If a rider were to ride right

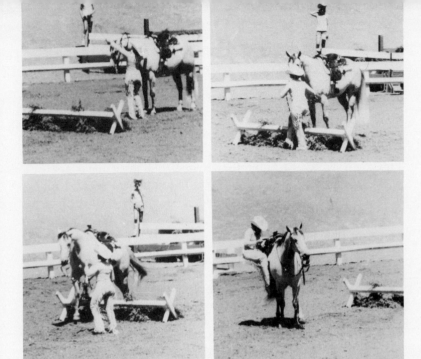

13.9. *The leadover jump calls for a dismount from the left side.*

13.10. *Linda tells Dandy to "whoa," making him stay until she is over the jump and has the reins correctly gathered and ready.*

13.11. *She brings him over the jump with a loose rein. No jerking on the mouth! It's a much nicer jump this way.*

13.12. *The judge said to mount on the right side after the jump, and Linda does just that.*

up to the jump and stop the horse, improper timing might cause him to try to take the jump with the rider aboard. You can see that Linda left plenty of room between Dandy and the leadover jump. She brought the reins over his head and gathered them up in her hands. Leading him up to the jump, she stopped him and made him stand while she went over. This gives a rider a chance to get everything organized before bringing the horse over. If the horse and rider jump together, the horse often gets his mouth jerked, and the rider might trip and fall; the whole thing can look horribly unorganized to a judge! When she was over, she loosened the reins and clucked to Dandy, who willingly came right over.

Next, the rider was asked to mount on the "wrong" side. This is an awkward move for anyone, but must have been especially difficult for Linda, who is only about 4 feet 11 inches tall! She did it well, however, and rode on to the next obstacle.

A sack of tin cans was hanging on a post, and Linda was aware of the fact that Dandy might be a little leary of the cans. This gave her a chance to gather him up well in advance, and use some left leg pressure to keep him moving in the

13.13. *A sack of cans is the next obstacle, and Dandy is taking a good look "out the corner of his eye."*

13.14. *Linda rides him up and takes the sack of cans off the post.*

direction of the post. Luckily, he stood quietly while she untied the sack of cans, and she was able to shake them noisily while carrying them. A rider who is able to "make some noise" with the cans is naturally going to score more points than the rider who acts as though he's afraid his horse will hear them move!

The next obstacle was a bridge which the riders were to go over while carrying the cans. Linda knew she'd have to hold the sack high enough that it didn't get caught on the bridge railing. At the same time, she'd need to drop Dandy's head by loosening her reins. She worked the bridge well and proceeded to the final task, hanging the cans back up on another post. Her entire course was well thought out, well worked, and, needless to say, she was in the ribbons.

Can you see, now, why you have to think out each detail? If you don't think about your pacing, your approaches, and the directions you'll be turning, you'll take a great deal away from the smooth appearance you're trying to convey to the judge.

13.15. While going over the bridge, Linda keeps the cans high enough that they don't get caught on the bridge rails.

13.16. The final task—hanging the sack on another post.

What is the judge looking for in each type of obstacle? The gate is almost always the first obstacle. A horse should move up to the gate quietly and be positioned to put the rider's hand near the latch so there is no excess reaching. If a horse is too far away, the rider has to bend way out of the saddle. This is the wrong way to work a gate. Bring your horse up and position him. If you're working the gate with your left hand, gather your reins up in your right hand, before you take hold of the latch to open it. Have a short enough rein so your horse can't walk off. You won't have to adjust your reins again until the obstacle is completed. When you open the gate, keep your horse parallel to it at all times. When the gate is swung WIDE open, ride up until your leg clears (or back if you're backing through) and pivot around, to put the horse in a parallel position on the other side. Sidepass in to close and be sure your horse is positioned so you can easily close the latch. You should have had your hand on the gate, sliding it across the top as needed, to show the judge you were able to work the horse and keep contact with the gate at all times.

Before you go on to the next obstacle, stay at the gate just long enough to reposition your reins. If they were in your right hand, shift them to your left and get them at the proper length to ride off.

What is the judge looking for on stepovers? A horse should pay close attention to what he's doing. He should show natural caution and should *care* about where he puts his feet. To give your horse a chance to work stepovers properly, cue him several feet in advance of the obstacles so he knows to drop his head and look. Whatever cue you use, whether leaning far up and out of the saddle, and putting the reins way up toward his ears, or just leaning slightly forward and loosening the reins, be consistent so the horse has a warning that he is to drop his head and look. When you come in for your stepovers, head right for the center. If you start them off to one side, the horse can easily duck off. If you start at the side, then have to leg him or rein him over to the center, you'll destroy his concentration and balance, and he'll hit the obstacles. Keep cuing him until he's well over the last stepover. If you raise back up, for instance, just as his front feet go over the last pole he'll raise his head, and this will cause his back feet to hit the obstacle.

When you're working backthroughs and backarounds, such as an L-shaped backthrough, your most important move is the approach. You stand a much better chance of working the obstacle with no mistakes, if you line up and space yourself correctly before you begin backing. The judge will not only be watching where your horse puts his feet, but he'll also be paying close attention to the attitude the horse shows. If he wrings his tail, gaps at the mouth, or locks up, he scores badly. If he quietly and willingly accepts the work and backs slowly, waiting for you to cue him, not "flying" through on his own, he'll score high.

Your mistakes could shoot down the chances of a good score when working a backthrough. Don't lean out of the saddle, shifting from side to side to see where you are. Using the L-shaped backthrough as a test, get properly spaced right between the two poles, before you start to back and take a look at each side to check your spacing. From then on all you should have to do is sit up straight in the saddle and just turn your head and look down with your EYES, not your body, at the inside pole. If you seem to be maintaining the same distance while backing, you're staying in the center. If you drift a little too far from the inside pole, you'll know without even looking that you're getting too close to the outside. Leg your horse back a little. While watching the inside, you can see the corner and you'll know when your horse clears the corner with his back feet. This is when you push his hindquarters into the turn, then carefully rein his front end around to back out. Keep backing until his front legs are completely clear of the obstacle. In most cases, because of the L shape, one pole on the backout side will be longer than the other. If you misjudge, and try to leave the obstacle too soon, you could turn and cause your horse to hit the pole. Keep backing STRAIGHT out until you know you're clear!

Bridges are generally included in trail classes. Remember to CENTER yourself on your approach so you go right for the middle of the bridge. With a narrow bridge, you particularly stand the chance of getting a stirrup hung up on the rails if you misjudge your center. With a bridge that has no rails, your horse is more likely to step off the side if you come on crooked.

Be careful of both pole and tire bridge combinations. One young rider told me that the hardest thing for her to learn was concentrating on each obstacle from start to finish. She recalled one class where there was a stepover pole just before and after the bridge. She worked her horse perfectly over the first pole, did a fine job on the bridge, then for reasons she's never really figured out, sat up in the saddle—the horse's cue he was done with the stepover—and caused him to knock down the pole while coming off the bridge.

We learn by our mistakes. A horse must often step into a tire when coming off a bridge. One rider told me of having a horse who liked to "hop" off the bridge, occasionally coming off somewhat quickly. She worked the bridge and, rather than slowly preparing the horse for the step-off tire, just gave him his head; he hopped over the tire and clumsily stepped on the rim. In this situation, she could have stopped him for just a second, dropped him, and made him see the tire, then ask him to step off. This does bring up the controversy of whether or not this constitutes a "refusal." In the larger shows, any hesitation before an obstacle could be ruled as a refusal. In the smaller shows, however, you should be able to stop your horse to look at a tire before coming off the bridge, or hesitate just a little before working a series of stepovers. I would NOT recommend a long pause such as walking up, stopping, dropping the head and waiting, before any obstacle.

Proper spacing is important when you must sidepass on an obstacle. You must always remember to space well, and not to rush the sidepass. It's not a race. Sidepass as carefully as you would on the trail if you had to sidepass off an obstacle you couldn't ride over and away from. Attitude is also very important here, and, if your horse pins his ears or wrings his tail each time you use some leg pressure, it's going to look bad to the judge. Keeping him relaxed and happy in his schooling will produce a horse that looks a lot more content on the show ring course.

What about spooky obstacles? Tarps, hides, waterboxes— there are dozens of spooky obstacles that you'll find on trail courses as you go from show to show. The fact is that even a horse that does everything well at home and seems gentle as a kitten is capable of blowing up at a show. You have to be ready for it. It might not seem spooky to you, but to the horse it's terrifying. Many riders become too trusting when it comes to trail horses, and don't have the chance to get instant contact with the mouth. If you're approaching a spooky-looking obstacle or you feel your horse start to get upset, don't panic, just gather him up with your hands and legs and try to get control of him before he gives you any real problem.

I've seen riders spend more time trying to get a horse near a spooky obstacle than it would take two horses to work the entire course. If you have spent a lot of time trying to get your horse up to something that he absolutely refuses to get near, and you know you've lost any chance for points on that obstacle, call it quits. One excellent trail horse trainer told me to NEVER stop a horse when he's scared. If you're in the show ring and the horse is blowing up, ride him past the obstacle, don't fight with him until you can get him to "go up and look at it." Sure, you've undoubtedly been told to never let a horse "get away" with anything or he'll be worse next time, but schooling is for HOME, not the show ring, in the case where the horse is truly afraid. However if it were a schooling show or small show, and the horse refused out of crankiness, then I would get after him a little and try to get him to at least TRY to get up to the obstacle. With a scared horse, however, you're only adding to the problem by forcing him up on an obstacle he's terrified of, especially if you've already lost points on it. Let's look at one reason why.

If your horse refused, for example, to ride up near a fresh hide (and many horses will do just that because of the smell) you would know quite quickly if the judge had ruled it a refusal. If you were only part way through the course, you would have time to ride him away from the hide and SETTLE

HIM enough to take him on and finish the rest of the course in a calm, relaxed manner. Just because you lose points on one obstacle doesn't mean you lose the class! If you overdid it, however, tried repeatedly to force the horse up to the hide, he'd become so rattled that your chances of working any more of the course without a battle would be down the drain.

You have to think carefully about how to handle a spooked horse. The hide situation is just one example. You can FEEL when your horse isn't going to quit spooking. Many novice riders clutch an object so tightly, and are so afraid to turn lose, that they chance getting hurt. A horse that's flying sideways, spooking away from something, is not likely to be watching where he's going—he just GOES. If you get in a "hopeless" situation then turn loose of the obstacle before you get hurt!

Remember, you must THINK about every move before you make it, and in the case of an unexpected situation, you need the ability to quickly think rationally enough to work out of the problem. Start your course with a strategy in mind. Listen CAREFULLY to the judge's directions, pay close attention to the posted course, and, if you have ANY questions, ask them of the judge or steward BEFORE the class begins. There is a certain follow-the-leader problem connected with trail exhibitors. If the first rider has a doubt and doesn't ask for clarity of how a certain obstacle is to be worked, he enters the ring and does it wrong. As a result, the entire class is liable to do the same thing! Don't take chances. Ask questions!

Chapter Fourteen

Tack, Appointments, Neatness, and "Turning Out"

As much as 20 percent of your score in a trail class can be based on appointments, equipment, and neatness. If the equipment you carry is wrong, you face possible disqualification. And what about your horse? He's being judged, in most cases, on conformation, which can make up another 20 percent on the scorecard. While you can't change his conformation, you can do several things to make him look his best and "dazzle" the judge.

Looking first at your horse's "preparation" for the show ring, examine his quality in comparison to that of other horses you've seen on the show circuit. Trail horses certainly don't have to be put together as perfectly as halter horses! Many trail horses, as a matter of fact, are a little on the homely side. If they have the talent, they can lack the beauty! I'm a firm believer that you can take most any horse, feed him, fit him, and groom him right and you can produce a very pleasant-looking animal!

First and foremost in fitting your show horse is keeping him parasite-free and healthy. Good hair coats are important in show horses and it's not easy to get a good coat on a wormy horse. We hold to regular worming schedules on our horses, and because we do this, we can feed them knowing it's going to the horse and not the worms!

A show horse needs a good grain ration to keep him his "shiny best." We feed various grains, but feel that one cup of soybean meal given once a day helps produce a good coat. This comes to about a pound of soybean meal daily. Oil is another additive you can use to produce a top show coat. Two ounces of walnut or corn oil added to the grain each day helps give the coat a beautiful sheen.

Regular exercise is essential for the healthy glow you want on your show horse. Many horses who aren't "conformation kings" can have their bodies greatly improved by muscle-toning. One of the major problems of the show horse is having excess weight added *before* the horse is toned and fit. It then turns to "blubber." We work our horses in a round pen at the extended trot and lope when it's a day to be worked loose and not ridden. Standing in front and backing the horse around the pen once or twice helps build the muscles in the hindquarters, a real benefit in reshaping a body. At the same time our horses are being schooled for showing, they're spending a lot of time being pleasure ridden in the hills. Often, we'll ride one and pony another.

If your horse is healthy and fit, your next task is to do the best possible job in "turning him out" at the show. This starts the day before the show with a good, complete bath. There are many fine shampoos on the market which are designed to bathe the horse without stripping the oils from his hair coat. If we wash a horse and he looks a little fuzzy, we'll put a sheet or blanket on him after he's dry and longe him just enough to get a little body heat built up. When "almost ready to sweat" the horse seems to secrete oils from the skin to the coat. After removing the sheet, we'll hand rub the horse.

Clipping and trimming, when thoroughly and properly done, can add *tremendously* to a horse's appearance. While the clip-

14.1, 14.2. *Tami scrubs Jack Gill from top to bottom the day before the show. Particular attention is paid to his white legs.*

14.3. *The ears, muzzle, and jaw areas must be clipped.*

pers are used the day before the show, the time-consuming job of thinning and trimming the mane and tail should be done ahead of time and not held for the "last moment." A good job takes a few days.

Most trail horses today wear short manes, four to six inches long. Hand-pulling produces the best, most natural look. After pulling, the mane might need some encouragement to lie down as neatly as possible. The neck looks more impressive if the mane lies neatly down on it—its shape and contour are enhanced. What can you do for "fly away mane"? One way is, believe it or not, to starch it. Make a paste out of dry laundry starch and water and rub it on the mane. Comb the mane down flat and lay a well-wrung, wet towel over the neck, leaving it there until the starch seems to have set. Leave the dried starch on overnight, then brush it out. If a horse has a white mane, you can even do this the night before a show, and when you brush the mane out before the class, there will be no evidence of the starch job.

When you get ready to clip your horse, be sure your blades are sharp and your clippers clean. Using a spray can of clipper "oil" will help keep the clippers cool and running properly. When you begin clipping, remember one important rule—clip only the side you're standing on. DON'T try to clip the left side of the head while standing on the right by just reaching under the jaw. It doesn't work. More than likely, it will prove messy.

The ears, when properly trimmed, can make a horse's head look much better than usual! Use your clippers to clean all hair from the inside of the ear, then go around the outside edge. Be sure to clean and neatly clip the tip of the ear.

The bridle path should be clipped as far down as possible. The horse's jaw, muzzle, "whiskers," and the hair around the eyes should be removed. By hair around the eyes, I mean the longer whisker-type hairs. You must clip these without losing any eyelash. One place often overlooked on the horse's head is the *inside of the nostril*. It's well worth the trouble to clip this clean, for it helps so much in producing that perfectly clipped appearance.

With a heavy-boned horse, or one who grows a lot of hair on his legs, we'll boot him two weeks before a show. He'll be

14.4, 14.5. *The end result is a well-clipped, clean horse, ready for his class.*

clipped from the knees and hocks down. Then, just before the show, we'll trim around the coronet band and up the back of the fetlock/pastern area.

When a horse is bathed and clipped, be sure he is put in a CLEAN stall the night before the show, and if the weather is cool enough, cover him with a blanket or sheet. The less time spent cleaning him up the morning of the show, the more time you'll have to ride and school him before his classes.

How About Tack?

Always consult your rule book for the rules on what constitutes proper tack and what is prohibited. For example, Appaloosa youth classes prohibit the use of riatas or ropes on the saddles. Other rule books have them down as optional, some list them as required. Let's look step by step at what you should have for your horse.

A properly fitting browband or split-ear headstall is essential. The bit should be of a "legal" type, as far as your rule book is concerned. In purchasing bits, the long-shanked kind might get you into trouble, if your trail horse is one who really drops his nose right down to look into the stepovers. If the horse's head is in an extremely low position, the bit could tap a pole, roll it, or knock it down off something else.

How about chin straps? The American Horse Shows Association rule book and most of the individual rule books stipulate the "legal" curb straps and chains which can be used. However, many of the shows, even when governed by one of these rule books, will add the phrase "no curb chains" on the entry information. The best way to play it safe is to have *both* a legal curb chain if you need it, and a legal curb strap, and you can put on the correct one, depending on the rules of each show.

Reins are more a product of local styles than anything else. The general rule on the West Coast is that you ride with romel-type reins. Other areas seem to prefer split reins. This brings up another rule. It is generally thought of as "wrong" to use romel-type reins and not carry hobbles. Someone came up with the idea, evidentally, that you can't ground-tie a horse with romel reins. Not only could the horse get a foot hooked up, but who wants to lay a good set of rawhide show reins on the ground for a horse to step on! The other general rule is that horses which are broke to ground-tie are ridden with split reins and hobbles don't have to be carried. I doubt if most of the horses being ridden with split reins are aware that this declares them as "broke to ground-tie." Nine times out of ten, the reins you choose will be on your horse because of the styles of your area. Keep to what is used in your part of the country.

Your saddle should fit BOTH you and your horse. If it fits you, you'll ride better. If it fits your horse, he'll work better, free of annoying rubbing which could cause sores. If you're looking for a saddle and want to try out a new one you see in a tack shop saddle rack, here's how you should try it out. Fold up blankets or something similar and lift the back of the saddle, placing them under the back so it raises the cantle area, much like the slope of the horse's croup area would cause the saddle to rise.

Next, be sure the saddle fits your horse. If a horse is wide-backed and the saddle has very narrow bars, it will sit too high off his back. The lower edges of the bars will dig into him. Newer saddles tend to sit a little high on a horse if the sheepswool lining hasn't been crushed down. This shouldn't be mistaken for improper fit. But you *should* check closely to see if the saddle is definitely wide enough to set right down on the horse's back.

The gullet, the area under the horn, should be high enough to stay up and off the horse's wither area. You should be able to stick two fingers horizontally between the saddle pads and the gullets.

Take care of your saddle! Do not leave it in your car trunk or a hot storage area. Heat is leather's worst enemy. It draws all the natural moisture out of leather, which can cause cracking and eventual breakage of parts.

Keep your saddle out of the heat and keep it looking its best by regular soaping with a good leather cleaner and conditioner. Before a show, take the saddle apart and give it an especially good cleaning. If you have silver conchos, a cantle plate, or horn cap, be sure your silver is polished. This also includes bridle silver. How do you get a top shine? First use a clean rag, and NEVER use the same rag on your silver that you use to soap your saddle. We use a silver cleaner, then rub and rub until the silver is "show-room shiny." The more you rub, the more shine you'll get. EVERYTHING must be clean, including your hobbles and riata, if you carry them.

The photos (see p. 256) show how to attach hobbles and riata to the saddle. The riata is tightly coiled, with the honda facing forward, attached to the right side of the saddle. The hobbles go on the left.

After completely cleaning your saddle and other tack, you might want to use one of the available commercial sprays we usually refer to as saddle wax. They give a new look to older saddles, producing a high gloss. Sprays are also available for last minute silver touch-ups.

Pads should always be clean and, above all, large enough to fit your saddle. A saddle with a 16-inch seat and large square skirt might not look right on a pad that's made for a smaller saddle. It might also chafe the horse. Whether you use a fleece pad, navajo blanket or other type of pad, it should be clean. BUT don't use anything in the cleaning which might stay in the pad and later secrete as the horse sweats. Bleaches or other laundry products might irritate the horse's back.

How about clothing? The most important thing with clothing is that it FITS you NOW. Parents shouldn't buy oversized

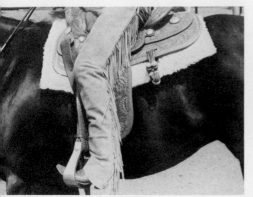

14.6. *Hobbles should be attached to the left side of the saddle.*

14.7. *The riata goes on the right, tightly and neatly coiled.*

clothes for their children to "grow into." Wearing well-fitted clothing is an asset in today's tough competitions. The sharper you look, the better chance you have of catching a judge's eye. Cuffs can almost always be added on to well-tailored chaps. Felt hats are now available in less expensive grades, making replacement or color change easier on the budget.

If you're a junior exhibitor showing in Western pleasure or equitation in addition to the trail classes, you'll no doubt be dressed a little differently than a person who only exhibits in trail classes. Equitation suits are popular for "all around" youth showmen, but you'll find the only real requirement for a trail horse exhibitor is a well-fitted outfit consisting of a nice hat, long-sleeved shirt, tie or concho pin, fitted pants (jeans are fine if they're clean), chaps, a nice belt and buckle and boots. . . . ALL of which should be clean and well cared for. Gloves, usually an optional item, add a lot.

How should a properly made pair of chaps fit? Across the rear, a chap that tapers in looks best. The back strap should actually be only three inches or so wide, so the chap becomes narrow toward the belt. The leg should be snug enough to look attractive. How you put the chaps on will have a lot to do with how they appear to fit. When you get ready to zip your chaps, be sure the fringe is set to go right down the back of your leg. If you twist the chaps while zipping them, they will bag at the knee, and the part which drapes over the top of your foot will be raised up and off your boot. Ideally, chaps should be buckled at belt height. They'll naturally slip down later. Any large adjustment of the chaps should be made on the back, NOT the front strap, or twisting can occur, even making well-made chaps look untailored.

Pay close attention to keeping your chaps neat and clean. Roll your cuffs up when walking around at a show. Don't let them drag in the dirt. When you mount and get ready for your class, hold your leg out of the stirrups and straight down and let someone pull the chap cuff down and give a light tug to get wrinkles out of the chaps.

When you store your chaps at home between shows, hang them inside out to protect the colored side from spots and stains. Never cover your chaps with a plastic bag, for leather needs to breathe. If you need to cover the chaps, make a slip-over bag of cheesecloth, or simply use an old sheet.

Remember that neatness counts. Everything should be spotless before you enter the ring. The horse should be well groomed and spotlessly cleaned. Your tack should be as clean as new. Your clothing should fit and be well turned out. A woman's hair should be neat and should also be kept off the number if the judge is to know "who she is." When you pin on your number, keep it even and pin both the top and bottom to keep it from flopping. These "little details" work together to produce a good image. Flying hair and a flopping number will make your horse appear "rough traveling" during the rail work. Even a fringe-backed saddle pad, on a horse that's not super-smooth, will make a judge notice your "bouncer." Pay attention to every little detail and look your best throughout the show!

14.8. A nice hat, scarf, blouse, and well-fitted pants and chaps make a nice "working outfit" for trail class showing. Pam has added a final touch by wearing gloves.

14.9. A "snow white" fleece pad, clean saddle, and polished silver reins and riata add to the picture of neatness.

Chapter Fifteen

Rail Work... A Necessary Evil

Rail work can often be responsible for as much as 30 percent of your total score. Some judges do it as a "formality" and seem to be busy scoring the obstacle cards while horses are asked to perform a very short span of rail work. Other judges go into it in more detail—in a class where several horses "went clean" over the obstacles, the rail work will be the tie breaker. Because you'll never know exactly what the circumstances are, particularly when showing under a judge you've never ridden under before, the only way to play it safe is to be prepared.

Rail work for trail classes is often held under different conditions than the normal pleasure class. The first time the Grand Prix trail competition was held at the Cow Palace, rail work was put in as part of the obstacle routine. Markers were set near the trail. Horses entered at the walk, picked up the jog at one marker and kept this gait until reaching the next marker, at which time the horse was to be picked up into the lope. Horses loped the rest of the way around the arena until reaching the first obstacle, a jump to be executed from the lope.

Another variation of trail course rail work over regular pleasure classes is the situation which arises when the course is set up on a track or other narrow area. At the California State Fair, the open classes are usually set up on the race track, and after the obstacles are worked, the horses go on the rail around them in this track area. Quite often, you'll be asked to do your rail work in a smaller area than a normal arena. School your horse at home to keep him sharp and ready for such instances. Horses worked in small circles are supple as a result and adapt easily to working in more confined areas. Horses constantly sent right down the rail in a huge arena, with only four corners to hit, become too used to traveling a straight line and even more dependent on "hugging the rail." In trail class rail work, there isn't always a rail to hug! Home-school your horse to work off the rail and not use it as a crutch. Circle him off the rail often; ride him straight down the middle of the arena; circle him in the center of the arena, working to keep your circles the same size.

The best way to find out how horses work on the rail in your area is to be a spectator at a few shows and watch the Western pleasure classes. On the West Coast, horses are ridden more "bridled up" and collected. Other areas ride with more

15.1. Check your area styles to see how your horses are "bridled." On the West Coast, horses are ridden with the poll elevated, and they "break at the poll" and set their heads in a vertical position.

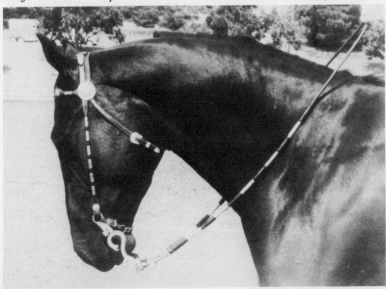

of a loose rein. Watch several classes, and try to see how the winners travel and how they're bridled.

Know What's Expected in Each Gait

The most important thing about each gait is consistency. By knowing what you need as far as how the horse should set his head or use his body, or how fast he should travel, you can set a precedence for your schooling, and work on getting the gait not only right, but *consistent*. Many horses, green to rail work, just can't seem to avoid "changing gears." Some work fine in arena corners, but speed up on the straightaway. You have to strive to keep the horse correct and at the same speed, unless you need to gather him up or push him on a little to get a better spot on the rail for passing or dropping behind a horse.

Let's examine the WALK. Some of the rule books clearly state that particular attention on scoring is given to the walk in trail class rail work. When a judge is scoring a trail horse, he's in a sense scoring a pleasure horse. He's looking for an animal that can be ridden out on the trail and cover plenty of ground. If your horse is capable of a good, brisk walk during the rail work, then school to "go after" that walk.

One exception to a good brisk walk is the horse that "single-foots." Since most judges are looking for a good, flatfooted walk, you don't want to have your horse passing all the others, singlefooting his way down the rail. Most of the time, a horse that obviously singlefoots when he's pushed on a little, can be collected up and slowed down to do a flatfooted walk. It *will* be slower than some of the other horses, but it *will* be a flatfooted walk.

If your horse can "flatfoot" on down the rail, use your legs to squeeze the horse up to make him walk with his back legs reaching well under him. Keep him "awake" in his walk, so he looks alert and doesn't seem to be falling asleep on the rail.

Most importantly keep the horse at the same speed, and *begin* the walk at the speed you want to maintain throughout that portion of the rail work. Don't jam him into a fast walk, then pull him down. On the same note, don't enter the ring with your horse dogging along at a crawl, then jab him up into a much faster walk. Learn to use some finesse with your hands and legs to put your horse right into a good walk and keep him at the same speed. If you feel him starting to break down a little, leg him before he has the chance to slow down. Leg him *easily* to hold him in his walk. Don't give him a swift kick, or he'll "jump out" a little and his movements will look jerky.

Going into the JOG requires a planned, graceful and smooth transition. Have everything ready before you ask for it. Take

15.2. *Consistency of speed is important. This horse is holding a good, steady jog.*

hold of the horse's head to gather him up, and check your own body position to see if you're sitting well in the saddle and can maintain a still body position for the transition. The only thing you'll be moving is your legs. If you lean forward when putting a horse into the jog, he'll tend to "leap" into it. If you sit still and hold his head steady after shortening your reins a little, then gently leg him with even pressure of both legs, he'll just "drift" gracefully into the jog. Again, as with the walk, you want to start this gait in exactly the same speed you'll be maintaining through that portion of the rail work. If you "jam" him into the jog, you'll then have to take hold of him and bring him back down. Try for consistency! It starts with the proper transition from the walk.

Work your hardest to keep a good body position and a STILL body at the jog. It's important with each gait, of course, but a smooth-jogging horse makes a judge use his pencil on the score sheet! If your legs are sloppy and flopping, it makes your horse look rough. If your body is swaying, it looks like the horse is making you do it, even if he's not. The image you're trying to put across is SMOOTHNESS. Keep still in the saddle, hold a good steady leg position, and when you cue your horse in, keep it as "secret" as possible.

If a judge is asking for quite a bit of rail work and not doing it just "to get it over with," he's liable to ask for an EX-TENDED TROT. The controversy of whether or not to lean up and out of the saddle during this gait, or to post to the trot, or to sit down in the saddle, comes up quite often. The best way to examine this question is to simply look at the fact that IF you can sit down and hold a pretty normal riding position in the extended trot, the horse is going to look "smooth enough to sit down on." Also you'll have an advantage over someone who is posting or standing in the stirrups, appearing to be in defense of a rough-moving horse. If you're sitting down in the saddle, you can still lean your upper body a little forward, if you feel you must. One advantage to sitting the trot is that you have complete use of your legs for aids. If you have a horse who must be constantly legged to keep his speed, then you're in a position to do it. You need good control of your aids to cue the horse "just enough" to keep him moving at a good extended trot without pushing him into the lope. Many horses mistake a rider's movement forward for a cue to move on. This is when a lot of horses want to break.

At home, we school our horses for the extended trot by beginning either in a large arena with a lot of straightaway, or out on a long, flat trail. With a lazy horse, I'll carry a bat or wear spurs. First, I'll put the horse into the jog, then I use a verbal command for the transition to the extension. A vocal command prepares the horse for what's coming with your hands and legs. I don't talk loudly unless I'm trying to discipline with my voice. Since I use a fairly soft voice command, when I'm in the show ring I won't have to speak loudly and disturb another rider's horse. I want my horse "tuned" to listen for what I say and you'd be surprised at how softly you can speak to a horse and still get a reaction!

Another advantage to using voice is the fact that when I ask a horse to "trot out" during early schooling, he learns that it means trot, not lope. And as I push him for more speed at the trot, he'll rarely break to the lope because I keep repeating the "trot out" command and he knows what to do. Once they catch on to this, you can bet they'll never break gait as long as you're talking to them.

When a horse isn't moving out as well as he can, and I'm using strong leg pressure on both his sides, I'll lightly pop him on the hindquarters with the whip—not hard enough to "jump him out" into a lope—just hard enough to wake him up. His head is always left alone during this "encouragement." It would make no sense to hit a horse at one end to ask for speed, and take hold of the bridle on the other end and ask for a reduction of speed! When you're trying to get a horse to move out, give him freedom so he CAN move out.

If you don't feel a bat will help move your horse out, spurs might help IF he doesn't get too rattled with them. Quite often, just lightly "holding" your rowels into his sides for a few seconds will encourage him to move out. Rolling or rubbing them lightly back and forth or up and down a little on his sides will also help wake him up. Don't jab at him constantly with spurs, or you're liable to produce an ear-pinning, tail-switching MAD horse!

When you school your horse for the LOPE, you have to school yourself at the same time. Most of the problems connected with the lope can be directly related to rider interference. Overcuing for the lope makes a horse JUMP into it. Rider error can cause a horse to crookedly travel down the rail. Let's look at what you'll have to do to get a good, steady lope.

No doubt you will ask for this gait from a walk. But you should also be prepared to take a horse into the lope from a jog or even an extended trot—this may be asked for at trail course rail work sections. No matter which gait you're coming from, sit down DEEP in the saddle and hold a good body position, with your upper body straight and tall, and your legs well under you. Keep your hand right over the center of the horn so your horse's head will be straight and he'll start out correctly, not bending into the rail too much. The only exception to this would be in starting a horse at the lope in an arena corner or on a small circle course where you'd have to bend him a little into the direction of travel.

As an example, let's take a transition from the walk to the lope, traveling counterclockwise, meaning the horse would be going into the lope on the left lead. First, be sure you have some contact with his head to "pick him up." Your left, or inside leg should be well under you. You'll cue him for the left lead by pushing with your RIGHT leg. If your other leg, the "inside" leg, accidentally swings too far forward (a fault with many riders), it will bend your horse and cause him to swing his rear end to the center and start off crooked. While you are pushing him off into the left lead with right leg pressure, you are "holding" his body straight with your left leg. It is held lightly against him, in a position where it is hanging well under you.

A good, still body position is also essential in the lope, as it is in the other gaits, because it makes your horse appear to be a smooth mover. A good rider can make a terrible mover look good. A bad rider can make the world's smoothest horse look like he's traveling like a jackhammer!

STOPS are sometimes called for from each gait, rather than just moving a horse down from an extended trot to a jog, or down to a walk. If you have to stop a horse right from the extended trot, he's likely to be a little "hyper" from having been moved out at such a clip. School your horse at home so that, no matter which gait you stop him from, you can hold him still without "undue restraint." Hold him with contact until you feel him settle, then loosen your reins. Don't be afraid to tell him "whoa" to hold him there, but be sure he's tuned into you enough that you never have to "yell it" in the show ring.

Rail Savvy . . . or Be Aware!

When you enter the ring for rail work, do it wisely. Remember, you're after consistency of speed and one way you get this is to start out by being well spaced. Let the horse going in ahead of you get at least three or four lengths out in front before you start in. If he appears to be a slow walker, let him get out farther than that. You want to enter the ring at a good, brisk walk and HOLD it. If you come in too close behind

15.3. Staying clear "on the rail" is important. Horses often do the trail class rail work in half an arena, on a track, or in a small area. They must be schooled for such work. (Yes, this horse is "laying into the bridle" and should be squeezed up with the rider's legs.)

another horse, you'll have to pull up some to avoid getting right at his tail. It's not always possible to circle down to get space when you first enter the ring, because there are other horses behind you coming in the gate. You can make a BIG circle, which will put you on the other side of the arena, where you will then come in on the other side of the gate. The best way, however, is to just enter well behind the horse ahead of you and stay on the rail, keeping a good steady walk.

The best way to show your judge how good your horse is on the rail is to KEEP CLEAR so he can SEE you. If you're lost in a mob, the judge will never see your horse. While you probably won't have much trouble staying clear at the walk, the problem will be more difficult in the jog and lope because the speed of each horse varies. Often a class of well-spaced horses at the walk will pick up at the lope and before you know it, they all seem to be on the same side of the arena!

Try to see how the judge is watching the class. If he is positioned so that he only judges one side of the arena, it gives you plenty of time to get a clear spot before passing him. If

15.4. This is especially good spacing for the rail work. Horses here are using all of the arena.

he's watching the whole arena, then you have to be extra careful to constantly stay clear, and in a big class, this isn't always such a cinch.

Let's say you're going down the rail and there's a group of three or four horses out in front of you. The judge is watching the class about one-third of the way around the arena in front of the "mob." If you continue right behind them, you're liable to wind up right in the bunch when you make your pass. Glance behind you and look for a clear spot to fall back into, and then start circling back to hit that spot. If it's close behind you, you can make a fairly small circle, but if you have to fall way back to get clear, make your circle bigger. Try to fall right into the spot you want, and stay there until you make your pass.

Corners are great for positioning your horse. If those three or four riders were some distance in front of you, and you were all approaching a corner, you could let them turn, then you could ride way in deep into the corner. It would take you more time to get around it than it took them. That gives them time to gain distance, and when you come out of the corner, they'll be farther ahead of you than before. This is another spot where a glance behind might help. If there was another mob coming up behind you, you might want to circle instead of dropping into the corner which might put you right back into the approaching mob.

Cutting corners also helps. A mob in front of you, which is riding to a corner, may have a clear spot in front of them. Before the corner, you cut to the inside, moving somewhat across the arena until you're out in front of the group, then fall back onto the rail. You've kept clear and done it gracefully. That's what counts!

Whenever you drop into a corner, cut a corner, or circle to get clear, be sure you know where the judge is. We had a tense, but somewhat comical moment occur one year at the State Fair when a young friend was using our mare for a trail class. The mare was 16.1 hands, very big and stout. The judge was fairly short, and, luckily, quick on his feet! The young girl found she couldn't rate the mare and slow down her lope to keep clear on the rail, so she suddenly decided to circle

15.5. Your horse should be schooled to stop and stand from any gait. If you have to hold on to him a little to keep him still, then do just that. As soon as he's settled, you can loosen your reins more.

and nearly "circled right over the judge." Yes, there could have been quite a disaster, but the comical part was the expression on the judge's face when this nearly 1,300-pound mare was coming at him. He had to jump out of her way *twice!*

Not only do you want to avoid killing the judge, but you also want to impress him, and part of that is done by showing a good attitude on the rail. Showmanship and sportsmanship are musts. Part of the rule of good showmanship is to keep showing that horse until you're out of the ring! Don't sit on your horse in the lineup, looking sour, or picking on him because you don't feel you had a good class. Hold him alert and stay "sharp." This doesn't mean you have to sit like an equitation exhibitor in the lineup, but it DOES mean that you should at least show a little "class" while you're waiting for the judge to turn in his score card.

Remember that rail work is often a tie breaker. In a class where more than one horse had a good clean trip over the obstacles, the percentage of points of the rail work DOES break the judge's tie!

15.6. Keep your horse alert in the line up.

Chapter Sixteen

Rule-Book Savvy

Imagine the heartbreak of having a perfect performance in a trail class, going flawless during the rail work, and being scored at the head of the class. . . . only to be disqualified on a rule-book technicality! It could be from a chin strap that is considered "illegal," it could be because your tack and appointments aren't in line with rule-book regulations. There are countless seemingly "little things" which can pull you right out of the ribbons, no matter how well your horse performs.

Rule books put the do's and don'ts in plain language and they also tell you what to expect. Some breed rules vary in different breed shows, and often vary from the American Horse Shows Association (AHSA) rules. The American Horse Shows Association publishes the rule book which sets down the "laws" for open, all-breed-type shows, and includes information from individual breed organizations. The breed rules are condensed, and there is much you should know about general *breed* rules that is not covered in the sections pertaining to trail classes alone. How do you cover yourself?

If you are showing in open shows, you should immediately acquire the association's rule book! If you have a horse showing in both open and in his individual breed classes, then you should have BOTH this rule book, and the rules published by the individual breed organization. This chapter will inform you of some of the rules and loopholes you need to know, but you should obtain the proper rule books for your breed. What is covered here is but a portion of what you MUST know to compete successfully. Let's examine what is covered in some of the rule books, what shows are looking for, what you can expect from the courses, and the requirements you should be aware of.

THE AMERICAN HORSE SHOWS ASSOCIATION

Trail horses must work over and through obstacles, without losing control; rider should open a gate, pass through it and close it. Other tests which may be required are: carrying objects from one part of the arena to another; riding through water, over logs or simulated brush; riding down into and up out of a ditch without lunging or jumping, crossing a bridge, backing through obstacles, mounting and dismounting from either side and performing over any natural conditions encountered on the trail. (American Horse Shows Association Rule Book)

Notice the words "any natural conditions." This leaves the course designer wide open for use of imagination in putting together obstacles, and you can bet that, in many cases, courses put together under the association's rules can be a lot tougher than the more simple breed-show courses. This is not always the case, but if you venture off to a big A- or B-rated show and compare the open courses with those of the ones used in that show's breed division, you'll no doubt see quite a difference.

The association's rule book provides illustrations of the legal and illegal curb chains and straps which can be used on bridles in shows governed by their organization. Some shows state in their entry premiums that no curb *chains* may be used. So at the same time a show is sanctioned by the American

Horse Shows Association, it may vary somewhat in its rules. It's up to you to know ALL the rules before you enter and show.

THE PALOMINO HORSE BREEDERS OF AMERICA

The rules listed under "Western Trail Class (Stock Type)" are rather short in comparison to some of the other rule books, but they do manage to list the types of obstacles that are suggested for Palomino trail courses. One thing that is different from many courses and breed rules is the TIME LIMIT OF TWO MINUTES to complete the course. Two minutes would barely put a horse through a difficult backthrough, in many of the bigger open-show courses. But this breed organization prefers a simpler course that CAN be done in two minutes. On a Palomino approved course, each horse is required to work at least five obstacles. This organization wants to see varied obstacles and states that "performance should be over or through obstacles particularly opening, passing through, and closing a gate without losing control of the gate." Other suggestions include carrying objects from one part of the arena to the other, riding through water, riding over logs or simulated brush, and, in short, the rest of this line which is, actually, the same line included in the American Horse Shows Association rules.

One of the highlights of the Palomino rules is the fact that these horses are judged ONE HUNDRED PERCENT ON PERFORMANCE. Other rule books state a percentage on conformation, performance, appointments and such, and this is often a sore spot with exhibitors who would rather see it judged the way the Palomino rules state. As with other breeds, the Palomino horses must perform on the rail.

Other parts of the Palomino rule book stress proper appointments. Though you're not being judged on "how nice your saddle is" in the trail class, you *can* be disqualified if you don't use the proper equipment. Here again, you must pay close attention to your curb strap. The rules state that "chain curbs are permissible but must be of a standard flat variety with no twist." No wire curbs, even if padded or taped can be used, and you can also be eliminated for using the wrong kind of *leather* strap. It can't be more narrow than one-half inch.

THE AMERICAN PAINT HORSE ASSOCIATION

This organization wants the class to be judged 80 percent on workover obstacles, 10 percent on rail work and 10 percent on conformation. This is thought by many to be a very desirable breakdown, because so much of the score is based on the work on the course itself. With the American Paint Horse Association (APHA) rules A TIME LIMIT MUST *NOT* BE PLACED ON THE ENTIRE TRAIL COURSE. The judge does have the option of setting a time limit on individual obstacles, but this might only be enforced if a horse was spending "all day" refusing one particular obstacle. The judge could then ask the rider to move on to the next one.

With rail work as part of the score, horses are naturally shown at a walk, trot, and lope and the judge *can* ask for additional work from any horse.

Six obstacles will be used on a Paint trail course. The association has two lists in their rule book, one of mandatory obstacles and one of optional ones. When the judge or show management makes up the course, they must include four from the mandatory list and two from the approved list. They clearly state that hazardous obstacles must be avoided.

To know what's expected of you when showing in Paint shows, you must have a copy of the rule book. Always read the other sections when you're showing in a trail class. The tack and appointments are set forth as well as "little" possibilities for disqualification, such as "The use of shoes other than standard horseshoes is to be discouraged and will be penalized by the judge." Such little known facts could keep you in, or out of, the ribbons!

THE PINTO RULE BOOK

Published by the Pinto Horse Association of America, Inc., this is a very complete rule book which includes not only the rules on trail obstacles, but some good drawings that are helpful in setting up a course at home or in the show ring. Part III, "Obstacles," is presented as a guide to the horse show committees to help them with the preparations for trail classes. By being familiar with this section, you can have an idea of what to expect or what NOT to expect on a course. It even includes information on heights and spacing of obstacles—a great help in setting up a practice course at home.

The Pinto rules allow a judge to use discretion in scoring on a percentage. The rules state that horses are "to be judged on performance with emphasis on manners, conformation, appointments and markings. Obstacle work shall count for at least 60 percent of the performance score." The words "at least" give the clue that the judge could score more heavily, if he so desired.

If you show in Pinto classes, you must also be aware of the rules under the section of Western performance classes, for these rules set forth the standards on acceptable saddles, bridles, bits, rider's clothing, and use of hands. A photo of acceptable straps and curb chains is included, and the statement that you can't tie a "cute little ribbon bow" in the forelock or mane of your horse because they are prohibited on Western horses. We often use the tiny bows on all horses from our barn at OPEN shows to identify the "unity" of our horses, but at Pinto approved classes, we leave them at home! This is another rule you have to read the rule book to find out about.

Appaloosa Youth Program Rules

The Appaloosa Horse Club, Inc., publishes two rule books, one a general show and contest manual, and one directed strictly to youth. There is a definite difference in the two, and if you are a youth exhibitor showing in both youth and open Appaloosa classes, you definitely should have both. Let's look at some of the youth rules which are different and more involved than the other Appaloosa rules.

In the youth trail class, the judge is not only watching the horse work the obstacles, but is assessing the rider's ability to put the horse over and through them. During the rail work, a little equitation judging comes into play, for the book states, "The rider's basic position in the saddle, hand position, leg position, seat position, and back position (as stated in the Western Equitation rules) will be considered in the judging."

Pay particular attention to the fact that, in an Appaloosa youth class, *no riata or rope may be carried on the saddle*. This would eliminate any obstacle requiring a youth to rope or drag a roped obstacle.

The course prescribed in the youth rule book is a timed course. It states that contestants shall have a time limit determined by the show management. The management also makes up the course which shall not exceed six obstacles.

What is the judge looking for in the trail class besides the judging of the rider's ability to put his horse over and through the obstacles? The rules state that, "A good trail horse should be a good pleasure horse with the ability to navigate obstacles normally encountered in trail riding." When rail work is done, particular emphasis is placed on the walk. This means that, at home, you'll have to spend some time schooling your horse for a nice, steady, ground-covering walk. A judge is naturally looking for a horse that isn't "asleep" and would be a pleasure to ride out on the trail—a horse that could "get you there" in reasonable time and cover ground. Whenever you show a trail horse, you're out there to give the judge what he wants to see, and particularly in a case such as this, which states in the youth guide that the judge should assign a point evaluation to each trail class obstacle, and should set up a point system on how heavily rail work counts when it is used. The rail work is never supposed to count more than any individual obstacle. Whatever the point system, the judge is looking for what HE wants to see in your horse and has the additional task of judging your equitation and horsemanship as well.

APPALOOSA SHOW AND CONTEST MANUAL

This is the rule book for classes other than the youth classes. The Appaloosa trail horse is judged on a set percentage of 65 percent on performance and manners, 25 percent on conformation, quality, and substance, and 10 percent on appointments. Similarly to the youth rules, the Appaloosa rule book requires that a good trail horse be a good pleasure horse with the ability to navigate obstacles normally encountered in trail riding. It also gives special emphasis on judging the walk and also on alertness and caution.

The rules state that performance should be over and through obstacles, particularly opening, passing through and closing a gate without losing control of it. They want their obstacles to be practical and realistic to assimilate actual obstacles and hazards encountered on the trail. If a course is set up with this rule in mind, it shouldn't be anything that will be "next to impossible" to work. While some shows have such strange obstacles that you wonder if you'll ever be able to work them, the Appaloosa rules strive to set up a course that is well within reason.

No actual time limit is stressed, but "Show management should give consideration to trail course design which will enable contestants to negotiate the trail course in a reasonable length of time." This is primarily taken into consideration because an extremely difficult trail course with large entries can take all day to judge and it stretches the show time out beyond reason.

Rail work is optional in an Appaloosa trail class. If it is used, horses work at the walk, trot, and lope both ways of the ring, and though they may be asked to reverse at the walk or trot, it shall never be asked for in the lope. Riders may be required to dismount in a trail class and, if an obstacle calls for a rider to do so and leave his horse unattended, it shall be optional to hobble or ground-tie the horse. This brings in the general "open" rule that if you ground-tie your horse, you ride with split reins and don't have to carry hobbles. If your horse is not broke to ground-tie, you carry hobbles and generally use romel-type reins. This is often a contradiction of "area standards." Nearly every horse ridden and shown on the West Coast has romel-type reins on his bridle, while other areas of the country often use split reins. When you're thinking about being "in style" you don't often consider the fact of whether or not your horse ground-ties or hobbles. With a trail horse, you should have him schooled for both situations, and this solves the problem.

American Quarter Horse Association Rules

The American Quarter Horse Association (AQHA) rule book states that the trail horse class will be judged on the performance of the horse at the three gaits, performance over obstacles, response to the rider, and intelligence. It is judged on a percentage basis, with 60 percent on workover obstacles, 30 percent on rail work, and 10 percent on conformation.

As with the Paint rule book, the American Quarter Horse Association has a mandatory obstacle list and an optional list. Three obstacles must be taken from each, giving a total of six obstacles for the trail horse to work. Only three obstacles appear on the mandatory list. These are: "(1) Opening, passing through, and closing gate (use a gate which will not endanger horse or rider). (2) Ride over at least four logs. (3) Ride over wooden bridge." There are ten obstacles listed in the optional list, three of which must be chosen for the course. They include such things as water obstacles, backing through an "L," putting on and removing a slicker, dismounting and leading the horse over obstacles not less than 14 inches or more than 24 inches in height. There are other obstacles in the list, and all can be made "creative" with a little imagination.

Hackamores, curbs, snaffles, half-breeds, or spade bits are permissible. Chain curbs can be used but must meet with the *approval of the judge*, and be at least one-half inch in width, and lie flat against the jaw of the horse. Rope or riata is optional.

How About Other Breed Rule Books?

Regardless of the breed of horse you show, obtaining a rule book from his governing association is relatively simple. Contact the following organizations for help in obtaining the rule book you need.

American Horse Shows Association, Inc.
598 Madison Avenue
New York, NY 10022

Appaloosa Horse Club, Inc.
Box 8403
Moscow, ID 83843

American Paint Horse Association
Education and Information Department
P.O. Box 18519
Fort Worth, TX 76118

International Arabian Horse Association
224 East Olive Avenue
Burbank, CA 91503

Pinto Horse Association of America, Inc.
910 West Washington Street
San Diego, CA 92103

Palomino Horse Breeders of America
P.O. Box 249
Mineral Wells, TX 79168

Pony of the Americas Club, Inc.
P.O. Box 1447
Mason City, IA 50401

Welsh Pony Society of America
P.O. Drawer A
White Post, VA 22663

American Buckskin Registry Association, Inc.
P.O. Box 1125
Anderson, CA 96007

American Morgan Horse Association, Inc.
P.O. Box 1
Westmoreland, NY 13490

American Mustang Association, Inc.
P.O. Box 338
Yucaipa, CA 92399

If after reading this book you would like information about subscribing to the magazine in which the individual chapters originally appeared, write to Circulation Dept. AR-10, HORSE OF COURSE!, Derbyshire Farm, Temple, New Hampshire 03084.

Suggested Spacing for Trail Obstacles

Walkover Poles:
Place poles 18, 20, 22 or 24 inches apart. The distances may be staggered, rather than spacing them all the same. Try varied spacings, such as 18, 24 and 22 inches.

Jog Over Poles:
The poles should be spaced 2½ or 3½ feet apart. The shorter space would call for working at a slow jog, while you would extend the trot for a 3½ foot spacing.

Lope Over Poles:
When loping, poles can be spaced at 6, 7 or 8 foot intervals.

In-and-out Jump at Lope:
There should be 12 feet between the two jump poles.

Spread Jumps:
Jumps should be no higher than 24 inches, and up to 2½ feet wide.

Backthroughs, L's, etc.:
Such obstacles should be 28 to 30 inches wide for the finished horse.

Jog Through (Forward):
The poles should be spaced 3½ to 4 feet apart.

Supplied courtesy of Ray Gillen, A.H.S.A. Trail Course Designer

Index

Agility of horse, 15
Aids used with tires, 139–141
American Buckskin Registry Association, Inc., address of, 280
American Horse Shows Association, Inc.
  address of, 279
  rule book of, 253, 271–273
American Morgan Horse Association, Inc., address of, 280
American Mustang Association, Inc., address of, 280
American Paint Horse Association, 274–275
  address of, 279
American Quarter Horse Association Rules, 278–279
Animals on course, 67, 212–215
Appaloosa Horse Club, Inc., 276
  address of, 279
Appaloosa Show and Contest Manual, 277–278
Appaloosa Youth Program Rules, 276–277
Appearance of horse, 248–255
Appointments, rules about, 273–274
Approach, teaching the, 153–154

Backarounds, 154–159
  judging of, 243–244
  on practice course, 60–61
Backing, teaching basic, 39–40

Backthroughs
  approach to, 153–154
  combinations, 159–163
  judging of, 243–244
  practicing, 53–56
  spacing, 147, 281
  training in, 147–153
  U-shaped, 159–160
  variations of, 153
Balky horses, 5–8
Barrel, sidepassing, 228
Barrels, backing, 154–159
Basics, 26–40
Bat, use of, 115–116, 265
Bits, 253
Body control movements, 26–40
Boredom of horse, 11
Bows in manes, 275
Breed classes, 271–272
Breed rules, 271, 273–280
"Bribing" horse, 114
Bridges
  in combinations, 43–45, 130–133, 189–192, 197, 244
  judging, 244–245
  for practice, 43–45
  sidepassing, 229
  teaching, 183–196
  teetering, 192–196
  varying, 185–192
Broke horse, 3

Cattle on course, 213–215
Caution, horse's natural, 15–16, 17